teach® yourself

windows vista

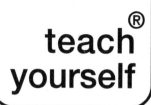

windows vista

mac bride

for over 60 years, more than
50 million people have learnt over
750 subjects the **teach yourself**
way, with impressive results.

be where you want to be
with **teach yourself**

For UK order enquiries: please contact Bookpoint Ltd, 130 Milton Park, Abingdon, Oxon OX14 4SB. Telephone: +44 (0)1235 827720. Fax: +44 (0)1235 400454. Lines are open 09.00–17.00, Monday to Saturday, with a 24-hour message answering service. Details about our titles and how to order are available at www.teachyourself.co.uk.

For USA order enquiries: please contact McGraw-Hill Customer Services, PO Box 545, Blacklick, OH 43004-0545, USA. Telephone: 1-800-722-4726. Fax: 1-614-755-5645.

For Canada order enquiries: please contact McGraw-Hill Ryerson Ltd, 300 Water St, Whitby, Ontario L1N 9B6, Canada. Telephone: 905 430 5000. Fax: 905 430 5020.

Long renowned as the authoritative source for self-guided learning – with more than 50 million copies sold worldwide – the **teach yourself** series includes over 500 titles in the fields of languages, crafts, hobbies, business, computing and education.

British Library Cataloguing in Publication Data: a catalogue record for this title is available from The British Library.

Library of Congress Catalog Card Number: on file.

First published in UK 2007 by Hodder Education, 338 Euston Road, London NW1 3BH.

First published in USA 2007 by The McGraw-Hill Companies Inc.

The **teach yourself** name is a registered trademark of Hodder Headline.

Computer hardware and software brand names mentioned in this book are protected by their respective trademarks and are acknowledged.

The publisher has used its best endeavours to ensure that the URLs for external websites referred to in this book are correct and active at the time of going to press. However, the publisher has no responsibility for the websites and can give no guarantee that a site will remain live or that the content is or will remain appropriate.

Copyright © 2007 Mac Bride

HGRN
3/08

contents

preface

Windows Vista is the latest version of Microsoft's worldbeating operating system, and one that takes another step further along the path of making computers easier to use.

Teach Yourself Windows Vista is written primarily for those people who are new to computers – if you have previously used any reasonably modern version of Windows (95 or NT or later), the change to Vista is very simple. This book introduces the basic concepts of working with Windows (the system) and windows (the framed parts of the screen in which programs run). It will show you how to set up your computer to suit the way you like to work – you can control more or less everything from the screen display down to the speed of the mouse's response! You will find out how to manage your files efficiently, organizing your storage so that you can find things quickly and removing unwanted clutter, and how to care for your disks so they continue to perform well for a long time.

The Windows package includes many accessories and applications, both large and small. We will be looking briefly at some of these, and more closely at Internet Explorer and Outlook Express. With these two tools you can browse and download files from the Internet, and handle e-mail. Windows Vista has been designed for easy Internet access, in fact, integration with the Internet is central to its design. If you choose, and if you have the hardware and the connections to support it, you can almost treat the Internet as an extension of your desktop.

This book does not aim to cover every single aspect of Windows Vista, for two very good reasons. First, there is far too much to fit into 240 pages, and second, few people will ever use all its features. *Teach Yourself Windows Vista* concentrates on the needs of the new user at home and in the office. It aims to cover the things that you need to know to be able to use your computer efficiently, and things that you might like to know because they can make using your computer more enjoyable. If you later want to learn how to get more out of your PC and/or set up a network for the PCs in your home or business, have a look at *Teach Yourself Home PC Maintenance and Networking* or *Teach Yourself PC Networking for your Small Business*.

Working with Windows is intuitive – once you know how to 'intuit'! When you have mastered the basics and become familiar with some applications, you should be able to apply your understanding of the 'Windows way' to any other Windows applications that interest you.

Happy Windowing.

Mac Bride
Southampton, 2007

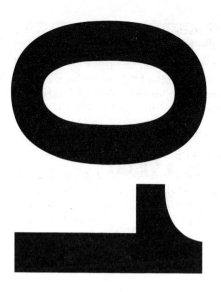

01

introducing Vista

In this chapter you will learn:

- how Windows Vista works
- about what's on the screen
- how to respond to and control Vista
- some essential terminology

1.1 What is Windows Vista?

Windows Vista is an *operating system* – and more. An operating
system handles the low-level interaction between the processor
and the screen, memory, mouse, disk drives, printer and other
peripherals. Windows Vista has *drivers* (control programs) for
all PC-compatible processors and for most of the PC peripherals
on the market – though in the first year or so after launch there
will be some Windows 98/XP peripherals that may not work
with Vista as their drivers are still being developed.

An operating system is a bridge between the hardware of the
computer and its *applications* – such as word-processors and
spreadsheets. As a result, whatever PC you have and whoever
made it, as long as it can run the Windows Vista operating system, it can run any Windows Vista application. (It will also be
able to run applications written for earlier versions of Windows.)

Although the operating system is the most important part of Windows, most of it is invisible to you. You don't even need to think
about how it works or what it does as Windows Vista has its
own routines for checking and maintaining the operating system.

The Desktop

The most visible part of Windows is, of course, the screen or
Desktop. Windows is a graphical system. It uses *icons* (small
images) to represent programs and files, and visual displays to
show what is happening inside your PC. Many of the routine
jobs are done by clicking on, dragging or otherwise manipulating
these images, using the mouse or keyboard.

Windows is *multi-tasking* – it can run any number of programs
at once. In practice, only a few will normally be active at the

same time but that is more a reflection of the human inability to do several jobs simultaneously! A typical example of multi-tasking would be one program downloading material from the Internet, another playing a CD, a third printing a long report, while you wrote a letter in a fourth.

Each program runs in a separate area of the screen – a window – and these can be resized, moved, minimized or overlapped however you like. Managing windows is covered in Chapter 3.

Utilities and accessories

Apart from the operating system, Windows Vista contains a large set of programs. Some of these are utilities for managing the system – organizing file storage on the disk, adding new peripherals or fine-tuning the way that they work. Others are applications for your use and amusement. You've got WordPad, a good word-processor, Photo Gallery for displaying images from your digital camera, Media Player for playing downloaded music files, CDs and DVDs, Movie Maker for editing home videos, a calculator, some games, a set of multimedia tools and applications for the Internet, including Internet Explorer, and a bunch of gadgets for livening up your Desktop. All of the essential utilities and the more useful applications are covered in this book.

Integration with the Internet

Windows Vista offers a high level of integration with the Internet – it can become almost an extension of your Desktop. Integration works best if your PC is connected to the Internet through a broadband line, giving fast, easy access – and preferably with the line open all the time.

If you connect through a dial-up line, you cannot move as smoothly from the Desktop to the Internet. In this situation, you will probably go online (connect to the Internet) once or twice a day to get your e-mail or browse the Web, and this will be quite separate from your other computing activities.

Multiple users

Under Vista, a PC can be set up for multiple users. Each user will have their own space on the hard disk for storing files and can customize the look and feel of the PC to suit themselves.

Plug and Play

These built-in control routines come into play when you add
new hardware, such as a joystick, printer or extra hard drive, to
your PC. Windows Vista will normally recognize their presence
automatically, and install the software needed to control them.
The 'plug and play' approach makes it easy to add peripherals to
your system.

The Vista editions

Windows Vista comes in five editions:

Home Basic; Home Premium; Business; Enterprise and
Ultimate. The core features – 90+% of the system – are the
same in all of them, but the Business and Enterprise editions
have additional facilities to keep data secure. Apart from
the Basic edition, all of these use the Areo interface. This
has some very fancy graphics effects, such as 'frosted
glass' borders to the windows, and 3D displays, but is the
same as the non-Aero interface for all practical purposes.

1.2 The Desktop

The screen should be treated as if it really were a desktop. This is
where you keep your tools – utilities and applications – and you
can arrange things so that those tools you use most often are close
at hand. This is where you create your documents – and you
may have several under way at the same time, in the same or in
separate applications. You can arrange these so that you can read
two or more at once if you want to compare them or to copy
material from one to another. If you have finished with an application for the time being, you can tuck it out of the way – but it
is still ready to be restarted with a click of the mouse.

What's on the Desktop?

What do you see when you look at the screen? The answer will
vary, of course, depending upon what you are doing and how
you have set up the system, but some or all of these items should
be visible.

Shortcuts   Application windows   Background   Sidebar

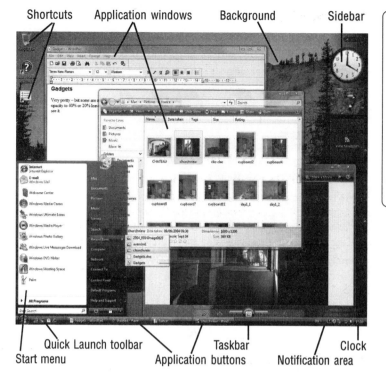

Quick Launch toolbar   Taskbar   Clock
Start menu   Application buttons   Notification area

Figure 1.1 The **Desktop** showing some of the main features.

Background

This may be a flat colour, a pattern, a picture or a Web page with text and images. It can be changed at any time without affecting anything else.

Shortcuts

These are icons with links to programs, to *folders* (for storing files on the hard disk) or to places on the Internet. Clicking on the icon will run the program, open the folder or take you off into the Internet. There are some shortcuts there already, more are available (see page 81) and you can add your own (see page 99).

Taskbar

This is normally present as a strip along the bottom of the screen, but can be moved elsewhere (Chapter 9). It is the control centre for the Desktop, carrying the tools and buttons to start and to switch between applications.

Start menu

Clicking on 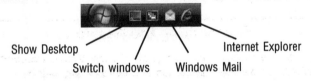 the **Start** button opens the Start menu. Any application on your system can be run from here. The menu also leads to recently-used documents, the Help and Support centre and other utilities.

Quick Launch toolbar

Shortcuts on the Desktop can be obscured by application windows, but the Taskbar is normally always visible. The Quick Launch toolbar is just one of the toolbars that can be added to the Taskbar to give you ready access to applications, no matter what the state of the Desktop.

Show Desktop

Switch windows   Windows Mail

Internet Explorer

Show Desktop shrinks all open applications out of the way so that you have a clear view of the Desktop. **Switch windows** offers one way to switch from one window to another (see page 39). **Internet Explorer** and **Windows Mail** are your main Internet applications (see Chapters 12 and 13).

Notification area

This holds icons for a variety of mainly system programs. The volume control is also here.

Clock

This is optional, but useful. The clock keeps excellent time – it even adjusts itself at the start and end of Daylight Saving Time!

Application windows

When you run an application, such as Windows Explorer (Chapter 7), WordPad, or Paint (both in Chapter 14), it opens in a window. This can be set to fill the screen or to take up a smaller area so that part of the Desktop is visible beneath (see Chapter 3 for more on windows).

Application buttons

When you run an application, a button is added to the Taskbar. Clicking it will bring the application to the front of the Desktop.

Gadgets and the Sidebar

On the right of the Desktop is the Sidebar where you can display your 'gadgets'. There are about a dozen of these supplied in the Vista package, and more are available online. They include a clock (and you can have any number of these, each set to a different time zone), a calendar, your contacts lists and utilities that will pull headlines, share prices or weather information off the Internet. We'll look at gadgets in Chapter 6.

Customizing the Desktop

The appearance of the Desktop and the way that you interact with it can be changed to suit yourself (see Chapter 3).

1.3 The mouse

The mouse is almost essential for work with Windows – you can manage without it, but not as easily. It is used for selecting and manipulating objects, highlighting text, making choices, and clicking icons and buttons – as well as for drawing in graphics applications. There are five key 'moves'.

Point

The easy one! Move the mouse so that the tip of the arrow cursor (or the finger of the hand cursor) is over the object you want to point to. If you point to an icon, and hold the cursor there for a moment, a label will appear, telling you what the icon stands for. If you reach the edge of the mouse mat before the pointer has reached its target, pick the mouse up and put it down again in the middle of the mat.

Click

A single click of the left button will select an object or position the cursor in a block of text.

Right-click

A single click of the right button will open a shortcut menu.

Double-click

Two clicks, in quick succession, of the left button will start a program or open a document. You can adjust the double-click speed (see page 126).

Drag

Point to an object or place on the Desktop, hold down the left mouse button and draw the cursor across the screen.

1.4 The keyboard

The keyboard is mainly for entering and editing text, but can also be used for controlling the system. Note these keys:

Windows – press to open the Start menu.

Control – used in combination with other keys for shortcuts to menu commands.

Alt – mainly used for menu selections (page 11).

Application – acts like a right-click, displaying the shortcut menu of a selected item (page 13).

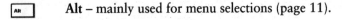 or 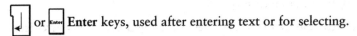 **Enter** keys, used after entering text or for selecting.

The first **Function** key. This one always calls up Help. The others do different jobs, depending on the program.

`←`	**Backspace** – deletes the selected object on screen or the letter to the left in a block of text.
`Delete`	**Delete** – deletes the selected object on screen or the letter to the right in a block of text.
`Home` `End`	Jump to the start/end of a line, or the top/bottom of a block of text or a window display.
`PgUp` `PgDn`	Scroll up/down one window length.
`↑` `↓`	Move through text, menus and folder displays. Can often be combined with `Control` for faster movement.

1.5 The Start menu

Any work that you want to do on your PC can be started from the Start menu (se Figure 1.2) – and many jobs can also be started from elsewhere, as you will see. The menu has been designed to give you quick access to things that you are likely to need most. It has three areas:

◆ The black buttons down the right lead mainly to documents, or rather to the folders in which documents are stored. Some lead to utilities, such as the Control Panel which you can use to configure Windows.

◆ The entries on the right are to programs. At the very top are Internet Explorer and Windows Mail, and these are more or less permanently fixed in place. Below them are listed those programs that you use most often. (At the very beginning, there is a selection of Windows programs here.) If you want one that isn't listed here, clicking *All Programs* opens a menu through which every installed application can be reached.

◆ In the strip across the bottom are the shut-down options and a special search facility.

We'll come back to the use of the Start menu in Chapter 2, and in Chapter 9 look at ways of customizing it.

Figure 1.2 The **Start** menu as it first appears – you may have a different selection of application links on the left.

1.6 Menus in applications

In any Windows Vista (or earlier) applications, the commands and options are usually grouped on a set of pull-down menus. They follow simple rules:

- If an item has an ▶ on the right, a submenu will open when you point to the item.

- If an item has ... after the name, a dialog box (page 15) will open when you point to the item to collect information.

- If an item has ● to its left, it is the selected option from a set.

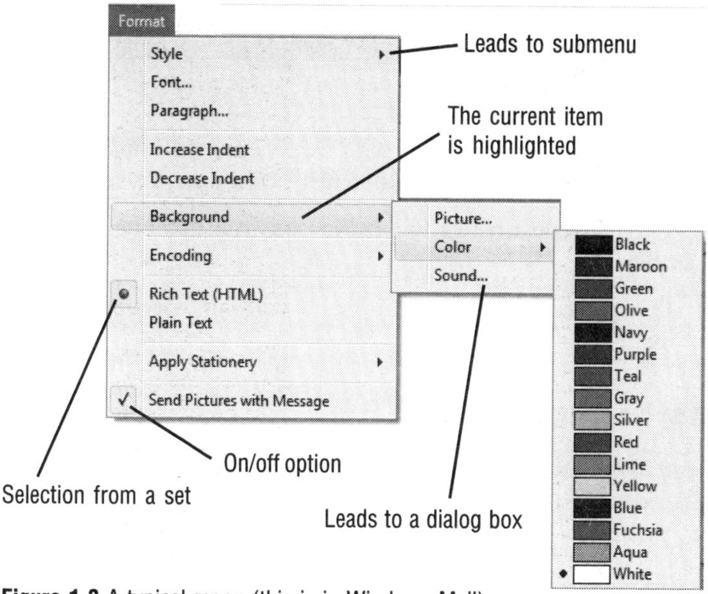

Figure 1.3 A typical menu (this is in Windows Mail).

Labels in figure:
Format
Style ▶ — Leads to submenu
Font...
Paragraph...
The current item is highlighted
Increase Indent
Decrease Indent
Background ▶ — Picture...
Encoding ▶ — Color ▶ — Black, Maroon, Green, Olive, Navy, Purple, Teal, Gray, Silver, Red, Lime, Yellow, Blue, Fuchsia, Aqua, White
Sound...
Rich Text (HTML)
Plain Text
Apply Stationery ▶
✓ Send Pictures with Message
Selection from a set
On/off option
Leads to a dialog box

• If an item has ✓ to its left, it is an option and is turned on – click to turn it off or on again.

• If a name is in grey ('greyed out'), the command is not available at that time – you probably have to first select something that it can be applied to.

Menus and the mouse

• To open a menu, click on its name in the Menu bar.

• To run a command or set an option, click on it with the mouse.

• To leave the menu system without selecting a command, click anywhere else on the screen.

Menu selection using the keyboard

When the work that you are doing is mainly typing, you may find it more convenient to make your menu selections via the keyboard. Here's how:

1 Hold down [**Alt**] and press the underlined letter in the name on the Menu bar.

2 Press the underlined letter of the name to run the command, set the on/off option or open the submenu.

Or

3 Move through the menus with the arrow keys – up/down the menu and right to open submenus – then press [**Enter**].

♦ The left/right arrows will move you from one menu to another.

♦ Press [**Escape**] to close the menu without selecting a command.

Keyboard shortcuts

Many applications allow you to run some of the most commonly-used commands directly from the keyboard, without touching the menu system. For example, in many applications, [**Control**] + [**S**] (i.e. hold down the [**Control**] key and press [**S**]) will call up the **Save** command; [**Control**] + [**O**] has the same effect as selecting **Open** from the **File** menu.

The shortcuts vary, and some applications will offer far more than others, but some are common to all – or most – applications. If a command has a keyboard shortcut, it will be shown on the menu, to the right of the name.

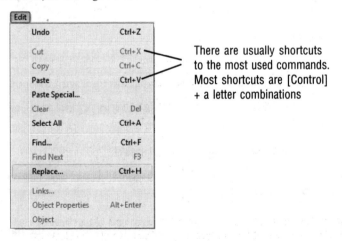

There are usually shortcuts to the most used commands. Most shortcuts are [Control] + a letter combinations

Figure 1.4 A menu showing keyboard shortcuts.

1.7 Shortcut menus

If you right-click on more or less anything on the screen – a file icon, a piece of text, a picture, the Desktop – or press the **Application** key when an object is selected, a menu will appear beside or on the object. This is its *shortcut* or *context menu* – it will contain a set of commands and options that are relevant to the object in that context.

Right-click on a shortcut to a folder, on a shortcut to an application, on the Taskbar or on the background and see what comes up. Don't worry at this stage about what the commands and options do, just notice how they vary – and that some are present on many menus.

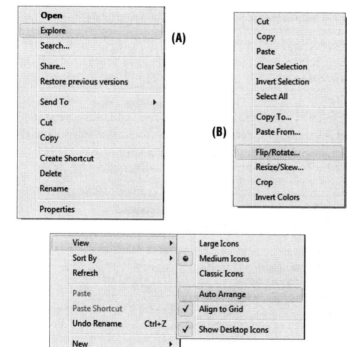

Figure 1.5 Three examples of shortcut menus, from **(A)** a folder in Windows Explorer, **(B)** a selected area in Paint and **(C)** the Desktop.

1.8 Properties, dialog boxes and options

Almost every object in the Windows Vista system has *Properties*, which define what it looks like and how it works. These can be seen, and often changed, through the Properties panel. This is normally reached through the context menu – you will see that menu A in Figure 1.5 has **Properties** as the last item (and **Personalize** in menu C also leads to several Properties panels).

Properties panels often have several *tabs*, each dealing with a different aspect of the object. The contents vary enormously. Some simply contain information – such as the size, date and other details – others have options that you can set in different ways.

*   To switch between tabs, click on the name at the top.

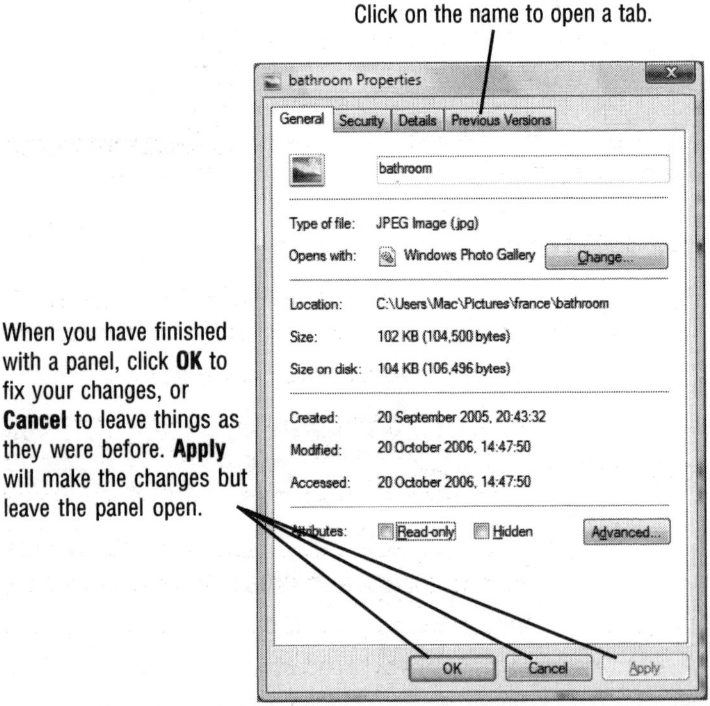

Click on the name to open a tab.

When you have finished with a panel, click **OK** to fix your changes, or **Cancel** to leave things as they were before. **Apply** will make the changes but leave the panel open.

Figure 1.6 The **Properties** panel for an image file. The tabs on some Properties panels are purely for information.

When a Windows program wants to get information from you, it will do it through a *panel* or *dialog box*. These vary in size and style, depending upon the information to be collected. Windows uses a range of methods for setting options and collecting information in its Properties panels and dialog boxes.

Text boxes

Typically used for collecting filenames or personal details. Sometimes a value will be suggested by the system. Edit it, or retype it if necessary.

Drop-down lists

In Vista utilities and applications, drop-down lists look like buttons; in older software they are more like text boxes. They can always be recognized by an arrow (▾ or ▾) on the right. Click on the arrow to make the list drop down, then select a value.

Combo boxes

This is a text box with a drop-down list built in, and the list typically stores names, web addresses or other data that you typed

Text box – enter the information

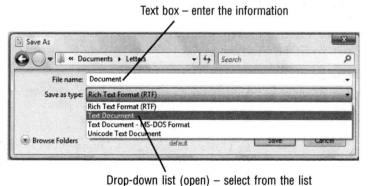

Drop-down list (open) – select from the list

Figure 1.7 A **Save As** dialog box showing a text box and a drop-down list.

in earlier. They are used where you may want to retrieve an existing name, address or whatever.

Lists

With a simple list, just scroll through it and select a value. They sometimes have a linked text box. The selected value is displayed there, but you can also type in a value.

Checkboxes

These are switches for options – click to turn them on or off. Checkboxes are sometimes found singly, but often in sets. You can have any number of checkboxes on at the same time, unlike radio buttons.

Radio buttons

These are used to select one – and only one – from a set of alternatives. Click on the button or its name to select.

Sliders and number values

Sliders are used where an approximate value will do the job, for example volume controls, speed and colour definition (actual values may not mean much to most of us in these situations!).

Clicking to the side of the slider will move it towards the click point, or you can drag the slider in the direction.

Numbers are often set through scroll boxes. Click the up or down arrows to adjust the value. If you want to make a big change, type in a new value.

1.9 The Welcome Center

This brings together links to a number of programs that you can use to understand and to configure your system. We will be looking at many of these during the course of this book – but if you are really new to computing, you might find it useful to run the Windows Basics link before you go much further. Click on an icon to run its program.

The Welcome Center has around a dozen items to help you get started with Windows – click the **Show all 14 items...** to see them all – plus a second set of links to Microsoft online.

By default it will run at startup, so that it is always there for you. If you find that you no longer want it to be there every time – you can get to all its facilities in other ways if you need them – click on the **Run at startup** checkbox to remove the tick.

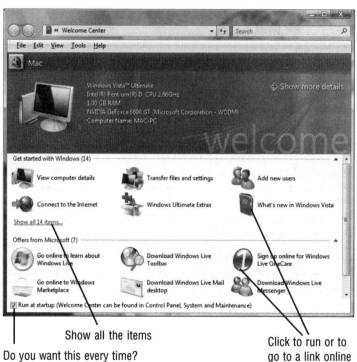

Show all the items

Do you want this every time?

Click to run or to go to a link online

Figure 1.8 The Welcome Center.

If someone else wants to use the PC, select **Switch User** or
Log Off and let them start work without having to restart the PC

Use **Sleep** to save power but leave the
PC ready to leap back into action

Lock to protect your PC when you are away from your desk

Figure 1.9 Turn off properly – don't just switch off!

1.10 Turning off

When you have finished a working session, you must shut down
the system properly – *do not simply turn off your PC.* Vista runs
through a shutdown routine that removes any temporary files
that were created by the system or by applications, checks the
system and closes down safely. If you simply switch off, you may
well find that it takes longer than usual to restart, as Vista will
need to check – and possibly restore – essential system files.

To shut down Windows Vista:

1 Click the **Start** button, point to the arrow on the bottom right
of the menu and select **Shut Down**. If any windows are open,
they will be closed, and you may be prompted to save documents (page 30).

Or

2 Hold down [**Alt**] and press [**F4**]. If any windows are open,
this will close the topmost one. Repeat to close all open windows, then to press [**Alt**] + [**F4**] again to shut down.

3 The **Shut Down Windows** dialog box will appear, click on the button in the centre to open a list of alternative endings. Select one and click **OK**.

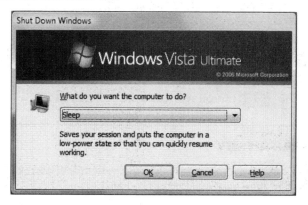

Alternative endings

If you share the PC with other people, or want to stop work for a short while, there are four options on the Shut Down menu which can end a session temporarily.

◆ **Switch User** suspends your programs, and allows another user to log in. It doesn't matter if they use the same programs as you have been using – the documents that you were working on will not (normally) be affected by anything they do. (There may be problems if the other users try to work on documents that you have left open.) When they are finished you can log in again and pick up where you left off.

◆ **Log Off** shuts any open programs, but leaves the PC running, for another person to use. This is the best choice if you have finished with the PC for some time, but others will want it.

◆ **Lock** suspends your programs and switches to the blue-green Vista screen. To restart, you must type in your password (and there's no point in using Lock if you haven't got a password). This does not completely tie up the PC – there is a **Switch User** option which would allow another user to work on it. Use this to protect your work from prying eyes or careless fingers while you are away from your desk.

You can also Lock the PC with the ▬🔒▬ button.

♦ **Sleep** shuts down the screen and hard drive, but leaves the memory intact. While suspended, the power consumption is virtually nil, but the computer can be restarted almost instantly. This is an attractive alternative to a full shut down if you intend to restart in less than an hour or so. Even in Sleep mode, a PC does use some power – the transformer is still active when everything else has stopped – but turning on and off frequently can accelerate wear on the circuits.

The [⏻] button will also put the PC to sleep.

Summary

♦ Windows Vista is an operating system with a package of utilities and application programs.

♦ The screen is referred to as the Desktop, and should be treated much as a real desktop.

♦ The mouse responds to single and double clicks of the left button, and to single clicks of the right button. It can also be used to drag objects across the Desktop.

♦ Certain keys serve specific functions.

♦ In any application, the commands can be reached through the menu system.

♦ Some commands have keyboard shortcuts.

♦ The Start menu gives you quick ways to start work.

♦ Right-clicking on an object normally opens a shortcut menu, containing relevant commands.

♦ Almost every object in the Vista system has properties, which define what it looks like and how it works.

♦ Windows Vista has a number of simple ways to set options and make selections.

♦ The Welcome Center has links to programs that you can use to understand and to configure your system.

♦ At the end of a session, you can shut down, hand the PC to another user, lock it up or put it to sleep.

02

programs and documents

In this chapter you will learn:

- about files and documents
- how to use the Start menu
- how to start from Explorer
- about file extensions
- how to cope with crashes

2.1 Definitions

The whole purpose of a PC, of course, is to run applications and produce documents – almost everything in the system is concerned directly or indirectly with doing this. So, before we do anything else, let's have a look at how to run applications, and how applications and documents are interrelated. But first, some definitions.

Programs

A program is a set of instructions, that make the computer perform a task. The task may be very simple, or highly complex. It is useful to divide programs into three types:

Operating system programs are run and controlled by Windows Vista – which is itself a program (or rather a set of interlinked programs). You are only aware of them by their effect. They manage the screen, pick up your keystrokes and mouse movements, control the transfer of data to and from the disk drives, prepare documents for output to the printer, and similar chores. Those of us who cut our computing teeth on older operating systems sometimes regret that Windows takes such total control of these, but overall, Windows does a good job of management.

Utilities are the programs that you can use to manage your PC. Windows Explorer, for example, allows you to organize your file storage (Chapter 7). There are programs in the Control Panel (Chapter 8) which you can use to customize the hardware and software, and another set that enable you to keep your disks in good order (Chapter 10).

Applications are why you use computers. They include business applications such as word-processors, spreadsheets, databases and accounts packages; graphics software for creating and editing images; browsers and other tools for communicating and working on the Internet and on local networks; multimedia viewers, players and editing software; games and much else. Most, though not all applications, will produce or display documents, and any given application can only handle documents of a certain type or range of types. We'll return to this in a moment.

Documents

In Windows jargon, a *document* is an organized set of information produced by an application. It can be stored on disk as a file and – typically but not always – can be output onto paper, to be read or viewed away from the computer. The most obvious examples of documents are letters, essays and reports created on word-processors, but databases, spreadsheets and Web pages are also documents, as are images, sound and video files. When a document is saved, part of its name identifies the application that created it. This association with applications is central to the way that Windows Vista handles documents. We will return to it in section 7.8.

2.2 Start ➛ All Programs

When we looked briefly at the Start menu in Chapter 1, we noted that the programs you use most often are listed in it. In fact, all of the programs already on your PC, and any that you install later, should have an entry here, under the **All Programs** heading. A program may be listed as an item on the main menu, or may have been grouped into a folder – which may itself have a further level of folders. These Start menu entries and folders are created by the routines that install Windows Vista and later applications. If you do not like the structure, you can tailor it to suit yourself (see Chapter 9).

To start a program:

1 Click [ ] or press [ ] on your keyboard.

2 Click on **All Programs**.

3 If necessary, click on a folder name to open it up – repeat as needed until you can see the program name.

What's ➛ this?

In this book, ➛ is used to link the steps in a menu sequence, e.g. **Start ➛ All Programs ➛ Accessories ➛ Paint** means 'select **Start**, from its menu pick **All Programs** then pick **Accessories** and finally select **Paint**'.

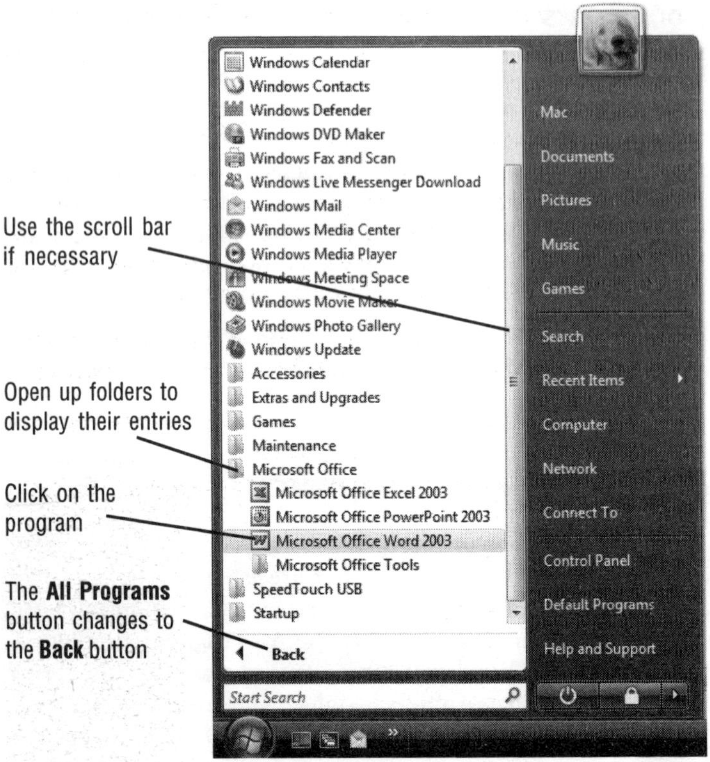

Use the scroll bar
if necessary

Open up folders to
display their entries

Click on the
program

The **All Programs**
button changes to
the **Back** button

Windows Calendar
Windows Contacts
Windows Defender
Windows DVD Maker
Windows Fax and Scan
Windows Live Messenger Download
Windows Mail
Windows Media Center
Windows Media Player
Windows Meeting Space
Windows Movie Maker
Windows Photo Gallery
Windows Update
Accessories
Extras and Upgrades
Games
Maintenance
Microsoft Office
  Microsoft Office Excel 2003
  Microsoft Office PowerPoint 2003
  Microsoft Office Word 2003
  Microsoft Office Tools
SpeedTouch USB
Startup
◀ **Back**

Start Search

Mac
Documents
Pictures
Music
Games
Search
Recent Items ▶
Computer
Network
Connect To
Control Panel
Default Programs
Help and Support

Figure 2.1 Starting from the **All Programs** area of the Start menu.

4 Click on a program name.

◆ If the Start menu has got very crowded, or there are lots of
entries in a folder, you may need to use the scroll bar to see
the entry you want.

2.3 Start Search

Beneath the programs area of the Start menu is a box labelled
'Start Search'. If you type part or all of the name of a program or
document, Windows will search through the Start menu – and
then on through the rest of the system – to find matching files.
Note that it doesn't just search through the names, but also the
content of files and this (in the pre-release version at least) can

produce some random results. However, it does find all matching programs very efficiently, and these are listed at the top of the display.

1 Click 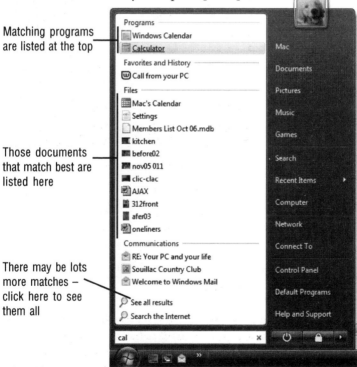 or press [⊞] on your keyboard.

2 Type the first few letters of the program name into the Start Search area – do not press [Enter]. Windows will start to match and list the possible programs as soon as you have typed the first letter. If you press [Enter] at any point, this will start whichever program is at the top of the list.

3 The programs display on the left of the menu will be replaced by a list of matching programs, Favorites, files and messages.

4 Click on the program that you want, or move the highlight to it with the arrow keys and press [Enter].

Matching programs are listed at the top

Those documents that match best are listed here

There may be lots more matches – click here to see them all

Programs
🗔 Windows Calendar
🖩 Calculator

Favorites and History
🔘 Call from your PC

Files
🗓 Mac's Calendar
📄 Settings
📄 Members List Oct 06.mdb
🖼 kitchen
🖼 before02
🖼 nov05 011
🖼 clic-clac
📄 AJAX
📄 312front
📄 afer03
📄 oneliners

Communications
📧 RE: Your PC and your life
📧 Souillac Country Club
📧 Welcome to Windows Mail
🔍 See all results
🔍 Search the Internet

cal   ✕

Mac

Documents

Pictures

Music

Games

Search

Recent Items ▶

Computer

Network

Connect To

Control Panel

Default Programs

Help and Support

Figure 2.2 Starting from a search. The **See all results** item will show you everything that matched – and almost all of it will be irrelevant, as the likely matches have been selected for display.

2.4 Starting from documents

Every type of document is – or can be – linked to an application (see page 110), so that when you open a document, Windows will run the appropriate application for you. The Start menu has links to those folders where you probably store many of your files – *Documents*, *Pictures* and *Music* – and *Recent Items* lists those files that you have been working on recently.

1 Click on **Start**.

2 Click on a folder or **Recent Items**.

3 Select a document. The linked application will start, opening the document automatically.

Figure 2.3 Selecting a document from the **Recent Items** list will run its linked application.

2.5 Starting from Windows Explorer

Windows Explorer is the built-in file management application.
You have almost certainly been using it already, though you may
not have been aware of that. When you click the Documents,
Pictures or other links on the right of the Start menu, it opens the
named folder in Windows Explorer, though it doesn't actually
say 'Windows Explorer' on the screen. We will be looking closely
at this vital application in Chapter 7, but at this point it is worth
noting that programs can be started from within it.

Running a program this way can be tricky – simply locating it
can take time. So why would you want to do this? Well, sometimes you have to. For example, if you download software from
the Web, it is often in the form of a self-extracting Zip file –
compressed and stored in a program. When this is run, it installs
the software onto your PC. That initial downloaded file will not
have a menu entry. To run it, you have to find it on your disk and
run it through Windows Explorer. And if you haven't changed
the default settings, it will be stored in the Downloads folder.

1   Open the folder containing the program file.

2   Click (or double-click) on the program name to start it.

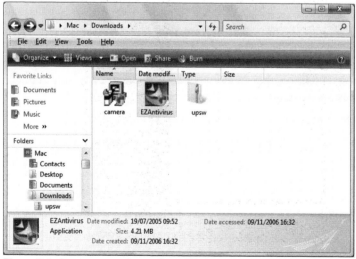

Figure 2.4 Programs can be run from Windows Explorer, though it can
take a while to find them.

Taskbar toolbars

Initially, there is only one of these on the Taskbar, and that is the Quick Launch toolbar (page 6). There are other ready-made toolbars that can be added – and you can create your own if you like this way of starting applications (see Chapter 9).

Desktop Shortcuts

Shortcuts offer a quick route to regularly-used folders and programs. When you first start using Windows Vista, you will find a few of these icons on the Desktop, leading to programs or folders. Click on a shortcut to run the program, or to open the folder.

There are half a dozen standard shortcuts that you can add or remove, as you like (see page 81), and you can create and add your own shortcuts to favourite folders and applications. This can be done easily through Windows Explorer (see page 99).

2.6 Filenames and extensions

When documents are saved onto disk, they are given a name which has two parts. The first part identifies that particular document, and can be more or less anything you want (see *Rules for filenames*, below). The second part is a three-letter extension which identifies the type of document. This is normally set by the application in which the document is created, and it is through this extension that Windows can link documents and applications. (We'll look at how to create these links on page 110.)

Here are some extensions that you are likely to meet:

- txt   Simple text, without any formatting or styling
- doc   Word document
- htm   Web page – can be created by many applications
- bmp   bitmap image, e.g. from Paint
- gif   a standard format for images on Web pages
- jpg   an alternative format for Web page images
- exe   an executable program – not a document!

Rules for filenames

The first part of the name can be any length (up to 250 characters!) and can consist of letters, numbers, spaces and underlines, but no other symbols. It's good sense to make sure that the name means something to you, so that you can identify the file when you come back to it later – and the shorter the name, the smaller the chance of making a mistake if you have to type it again.

Standard formats

Life would be easier if there was only one standard format for each type of document, but instead there are loads of them, especially for word-processing and graphics. You might wonder why. According to the old joke, computer people love standards – which is why they have so many. In fact, there are several reasons. When a software house develops a new application, or a new version of an existing one, it will sometimes use a different document format – partly to handle its special features, and partly to distinguish it from its rivals. Some formats are developed to meet

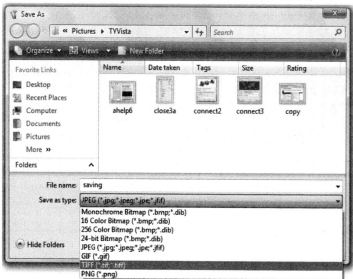

Figure 2.5 A typical **Save As** dialog box. This one is from Paint which can save in several formats. All programs have their native format, and many can import or export files in other formats for transfer between programs.

particular needs. With graphics documents, for instance, there is a trade-off between file size and image quality, and formats have been developed across the range.

The extension must match the application. As a general rule, when you save a file for the first time, simply give the identifying name and let the application set the extension. If the application can output documents in different formats, and you know that you need a particular format, select it from the **Save as type** list. After the first save, the filename is set, though the file could be later saved under a different name and in a different format. You might, for example, have edited a Word document to make it into a Web page, and so need to save it as an HTML file.

2.7 Closing programs

When you have finished using an application, it must be closed down properly.
Closing its window (page 44) will close
the program, but you will also find a
Close or **Exit** option on the **File** menu.
The key combination [**Alt**] + [**F4**] also
closes applications.

If you have created or edited a file, and not saved the changes, you will be prompted to save before the application closes.

* Select **Yes** to save.

* Select **No** to exit without saving.

* Select **Cancel** to return
to the application.

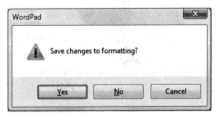

The double-check

Whenever you do anything which could be potentially dangerous to the system, Vista will ask you to confirm. This is a safety feature. It is there in case a rogue program got into your PC and tried to change the settings or delete files.

2.8 Coping with crashes

Vista is more reliable and robust than earlier versions of Windows, but software is rarely perfect. Some applications – and some combinations of applications – are more likely than others to crash. If you are interested, crashes are normally caused by two programs trying to use the same area of memory, and you can go find a big technical book if you want to know more! If you are lucky, you won't have crashes often. But just in case...

If you see any of these, your PC has probably crashed.

- The busy symbol appears and stays (but wait twice as long as normal just in case it has more to do than you thought).
- No response to key presses or mouse actions.
- The screen does not display properly – there might be part of a window or dialog box left behind and unmovable.

This will often solve the problem:

1 Press these keys: [Ctrl] [Alt] and [Delete]. The Desktop will be replaced by the green-blue screen, with the options:

    Lock this computer

    Switch User

    Log off

    Change a password

    Start Task Manager.

2 Click **Start Task Manager**. The **Task Manager** dialog box will appear. Open the **Applications** tab if it is not already open. The program that has crashed should be at the top of the list – with 'Not responding' after the name.

3 If an application is not responding, click **End Task** – and confirm when prompted. The system should work properly once it is out of the way.

4 If the highlighted program is *not* marked 'Not responding', it probably hasn't crashed – click X to close Task Manager and give Windows a bit longer to sort itself out.

Figure 2.6 The Task Manager dialog box open at the **Applications** tab.

Summary

- There are three main types of programs: operating system, utilities and applications.

- The data files produced by or displayed by applications are called documents.

- Programs can be started from the Start menu, the Taskbar or from within Windows Explorer.

- Opening a document will run its associated application.

- Programs should be closed down properly when you have finished using them.

- Filenames have two parts: an identifying name and an extension which describes the format of the file.

- If a program crashes, the **[Ctrl] + [Alt] + [Delete]** key combination will take you to a screen where you can open the Task Manager dialog box.

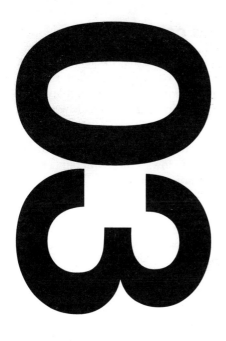

03

working with windows

In this chapter you will learn:

- about windows, frames and their controls
- about screen layouts
- how to switch between windows
- how to resize and move windows

3.1 Basic windows concepts

A window is a framed area of the screen that exists and is controlled independently of any other windows. All applications are displayed in windows. If an application can handle multiple documents, they may each be displayed in their own window within the application.

If you only use one application at a time, you don't have to think too much about managing your windows – there will only be the one. But this kind of usage does not take advantage of Windows Vista, which is a multi-tasking system. If you are going to have several applications open at once, you must know how to switch between them, and how to arrange their windows so that you can work efficiently. This chapter will show you how.

A window normally has these features:

* A **Title bar** showing the name of the application and the current document;

* **Minimize**, **Maximize** and **Close** buttons on the far right of the title bar – for changing the mode (page 35) and for shutting down;

* An icon at the far left of the Title Bar – leading to the window's **Control menu** (page 36);

* **Scroll bars** along the right and bottom – for moving the contents within the frame. These are only present if the contents are too wide or too long to fit within the frame.

* A thin outer **border** – for changing the window size (page 41).

How many windows at once?

There is no fixed limit to the number of windows that you can have open at the same time. The maximum depends on the amount of RAM on the computer and how memory-hungry the applications are. I have had 30 applications running simultaneously, though 26 of these were started accidentally! (Don't lean on the **Enter** key when an application icon is selected on the Desktop...)

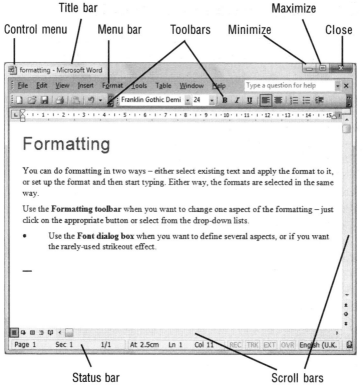

Title bar

Control menu / Menu bar / Toolbars / Minimize / Maximize / Close

formatting - Microsoft Word

File   Edit   View   Insert   Format   Tools   Table   Window   Help   Type a question for help

Franklin Gothic Demi   24   **B**   *I*   U

Formatting

You can do formatting in two ways – either select existing text and apply the format to it, or set up the format and then start typing. Either way, the formats are selected in the same way.

Use the **Formatting toolbar** when you want to change one aspect of the formatting – just click on the appropriate button or select from the drop-down lists.

* Use the **Font dialog box** when you want to define several aspects, or if you want the rarely-used strikeout effect.

Page 1   Sec 1   1/1   At 2.5cm   Ln 1   Col 11   REC   TRK   EXT   OVR   English (U.K.)

Status bar   Scroll bars

Figure 3.1 The main features of windows.

Application windows also have:

* **Menu bar** – leading to the full set of commands and options;

* One or more **Toolbars** – containing icons that call up the more commonly-used commands and options. Toolbars are normally along the top of the working area, but may be down either side, or as 'floating' panels anywhere on screen.

* The **Status bar** – displaying a variety of information about the current activity in the application.

Both application and document windows can be in one of three modes, and the simplest way to switch them is with the buttons at the top right:

Minimize – An application is then visible only as a button on the Taskbar. A minimized document is reduced so that only the Title bar and window control buttons are visible.

Maximize – An application window fills the screen and loses its outer frame. When a document is maximized in its application's working area, its Title bar is merged with the application Title bar and its window control buttons are placed on the far right of the Menu bar.

Restore – The window is smaller than the full screen or working area. Its size can be adjusted, and it can be moved to any position – within or beyond the limits of the screen.

Restore is on the **Maximize** button in a maximized window, and on the **Minimize** button of a minimized window.

The Control menu

This can be opened by clicking the icon at the far left of the Title bar. But this is really here for keyboard users.

Press **Alt** and the **Space bar** to open the menu in applications, or **Alt** and the **Minus** key in documents.

You can now Mi<u>n</u>imize, Ma<u>x</u>imize/ <u>R</u>estore or <u>C</u>lose by pressing the keys of the underlined letters. (**Alt + F4** is a shortcut for Close.)

This is also where keyboard users start to <u>M</u>ove (page 43) or change the <u>S</u>ize (page 42) of the window.

3.2 Using the scroll bars

When you are working on a large picture or a long document, only the part that you are working on will be displayed within the window. Scroll bars will be present along the bottom and/or right of the frame and can be used to move the hidden parts of the document into the working area. They can be controlled in three ways:

- Click on the arrows at the ends to nudge the contents in the direction of the arrow – typically the movement will be a line or so at a time, but the amount of movement varies with the application and document size.

- Click on the bar to the side of or above or below the slider for a larger movement – typically just less than the height or width of the working area.

- Drag the slider. This is the quickest way to scroll through a large document.

Small movement

Large movement   Slider – drag as needed

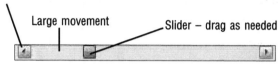

Automatic scrolling

If the typing, drawing or other movements that you make while working on your document take the current position out of the visible area, the document will be scrolled automatically to bring the current position back into view.

3.3 Screen layouts

Windows Vista allows you enormous flexibility in your screen layouts, though the simplest layout that will do the job is usually the best. You can only ever work on one application at a time – but that is a limitation of humans, not computers. However, you can copy or move files or data between two windows and there may be continuing activities, such as printing or downloading, going on in other windows. If you do not actually need to see what is happening in the other windows, the simplest layout is to run all applications in Maximized mode. The one that you are working on will fill the screen, obscuring the others, but you can easily bring one of those to the front by clicking on its button in the Taskbar.

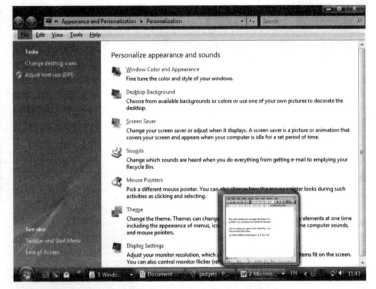

Figure 3.2 If you are only working on one application, you may as well run it in a Maximized window and have the largest working/viewing area. Other windows can be reached, when needed, through their Taskbar buttons.

Multiple window layouts

Sometimes you will want to be able to see two or more windows at the same time – perhaps to copy material from one application to another. The simplest approach here is to use one of the commands for arranging windows.

• **Cascade Windows** will take all windows currently open on the screen and arrange them so they overlap neatly.

• **Show Windows Stacked** arranges them one above the other – going to two columns if there are more than three windows.

• **Show Windows Side by Side** arranges them in vertical strips – but going to two rows with more than three windows.

1 Check that all the windows you want to include in the display are in Maximized or Restore mode.

2 Right-click on a blank area of the Taskbar.

3 Select a **Cascade** or **Show Windows...** command.

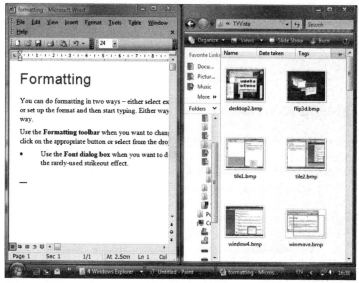

Figure 3.3 The **Tile** displays work better with bigger screens. An 800 × 600 screen can cope with two windows – more at a pinch.

4   When you want to return to the previous layout, right-click the Taskbar. The menu will now have an **Undo Cascade** or **Undo Show Windows...** command.

3.4   Switching between windows

You can only work in the active window – the topmost one. And if you've got a pile-up and can't quite work out which one is on top, the Close button in the top right of the active window is red ![x] not blue ![x] (shame this book isn't in colour). So, when you want to work in an open window, the first thing to do is bring it to the top.

There are two simple ways to bring a window to the top:

- If you can see any part of the window, click on it.
- Click on its Taskbar button – it is labelled and a thumbnail image of the window will appear when you point to it.

Tabbing to windows

Sometimes you cannot see the window you want to reach, and switching between windows by using their Taskbar buttons is not always convenient. Here is a neat alternative:

1 Hold down [**Alt**] and press [**Tab**]. This panel appears.

Welcome Center

2 Press [**Tab**] again until the application that you want is highlighted – if you go off the end, it cycles back to the start.

3 Release [**Alt**]. The selected window will come to the front.

Flip 3D

If you have the Windows Aero display, there is a rather flash graphic method for switching between windows, called Flip 3D. This displays all open windows – including those minimized onto the Taskbar – sideways on and reduced in size, but clear enough to be able to see what is happening. You can cycle through them, bringing each to the front in turn, where it is larger and easier to see, until you find the one you want.

1 Hold down the [**Windows**] key and press [**Tab**].

2 Repeat Step 1. The windows will cycle round from left to right, with the one at the front going to the back of the queue.

3 When the one you want is at the front, release [**Windows**].

Figure 3.4 Using Flip 3D to switch to another window.

3.5 Adjusting the window size

When a window is in Restore mode, its size can be adjusted freely. This can be done easily with the mouse or – less easily – with the keyboard.

Using the mouse

1 Select the document or application window.

2 Point to an edge or corner of the frame – when you are in a suitable place the cursor changes to a double-headed arrow.

3 Hold down the left button and drag an edge or a corner to change the window size. If the **Show windows contents while dragging** option is on, the window will change size as you drag. If this option is off, you will see an outline showing the new window size. (To set this option, see page 74.)

4 Release the mouse button.

5 Repeat on other edges or corners if necessary.

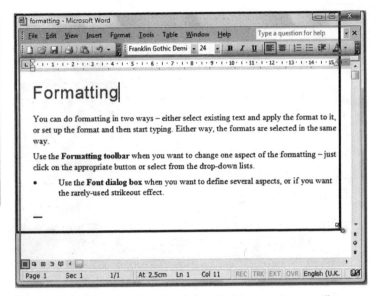

Figure 3.5 Adjusting the size of a window. In this example, an outline shows the new size as *Show windows contents while dragging* has been turned off. It can be more efficient to change the size by dragging a corner, rather than an edge, but it is trickier to locate the cursor at the start.

Using the keyboard

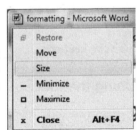

1 Open the Control menu. Hold down [**Alt**] and press [**Space bar**] in an application, or [**Alt**] + [**-**] (minus) in a document.

2 Press **S** to select Size.

3 Press the arrow key corresponding to the edge that you want to move. A double-headed arrow will appear on that edge.

4 Use the arrow keys to move the edge into its new position.

5 Press **Enter** to fix the new size.

6 Repeat for the other edges or corners if necessary.

3.6 Moving windows

A window in Restore mode can be moved to anywhere on – or part-ways off – the screen. The Title bar is the 'handle' for movement. In those applications that display documents in their own windows, these windows can be moved around the working area of the application in exactly the same way.

Moving with the mouse

*   Point to anywhere on the Title bar and drag the window to its new place.

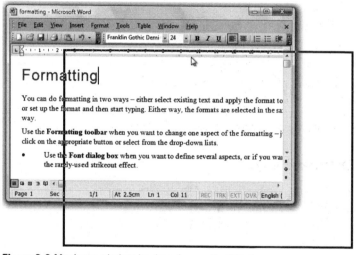

Figure 3.6 Moving a window by dragging on the Title bar.

Moving with the keyboard

1   Open the Control menu and select **Move**.

2   Use the arrow keys to move the window as required.

3   Press **Enter** to fix the new position.

3.7 Closing windows

When you have finished with a window, close it. This will free up memory so that other applications run more smoothly, as well as reducing the clutter on your Desktop.

There are three methods which will work with any window:

• Click the **Close** button  in the top right corner.

• Hold down **Alt** and press [-] (the minus key) to open the Control menu and select **Close**.

⬓	Restore	
	Move	
	Size	
▬	Minimize	
◻	Maximize	
x	**Close**	**Alt+F4**

• Hold down the **Alt** key and press [**F4**].

Exit and close

You can also close a window by exiting from an application (see section 2.7, *Closing programs*, page 30).

Summary

* Windows can be open in Maximized, Restore or Minimized modes.

* To switch between the display modes, use the control buttons on the top right of the frame, or the commands on the Control menu.

* If the contents of a window go beyond the boundaries of the frame, the scroll bars can be used to pull distant areas into view.

* There are many different ways to arrange windows on your screen – the simplest is to work with all windows Maximized, pulling them to the front as needed.

* The Cascade and Show Windows arrangements will display (part of) all the windows in Maximized and Restore mode.

* You can switch between open windows by holding down [Alt] and pressing [Tab].

* With Aero systems, you can flip through graphics of each window by holding down [Windows] and pressing [Tab].

* The size of a window can be changed by dragging on an edge or corner, or using the Control menu Size command and the arrow keys.

* Windows can be moved by dragging on their Title bar, or with the Control menu Move command.

* Windows should be closed when no longer needed to reduce screen clutter and free up memory.

04

basic skills

In this chapter you will learn:

- how to select text and objects
- how to cut, copy and paste data
- about drag and drop
- about scraps

4.1   Selection techniques

Before you can do any work on an object or a set of objects – e.g. format a block of text, copy part of an image, move a group of files from one folder to another – you must select it.

Text

Use WordPad or any word-processor to try out these techniques. They can also be used with text objects in graphics packages and even with small items of text such as filenames.

With the mouse:

1   Point to the start of the text.

2   Hold down the left mouse button and drag across the screen.

3   The selected text will be highlighted.

With the keyboard:

1   Move the cursor to the start of the text.

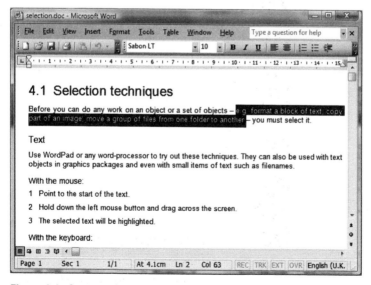

Figure 4.1 Once text has been selected, it can be edited, copied, moved, deleted or formatted.

2 Hold down [**Shift**].

3 Use the arrow keys to highlight the text you want.

Graphics

The same techniques are used for images in graphics applications, and for icons on the Desktop, files in Computer and other screen objects.

Single object:

• Point to it. If this does not highlight it, click on it.

Adjacent objects:

1 Imagine a rectangle that will enclose the objects.

2 Point to one corner of this rectangle.

3 Hold down the left mouse button and drag across to the opposite corner – an outline will appear as you do this.

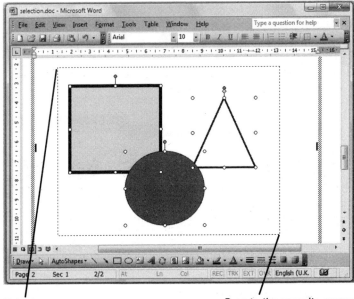

Point to one corner   Drag to the opposite corner

Figure 4.2 Selecting drawn objects.

Or where the objects are in a set, e.g. the icons and files

4 Select the object at one corner.

5 Hold down [**Shift**] and click on the object at the opposite corner.

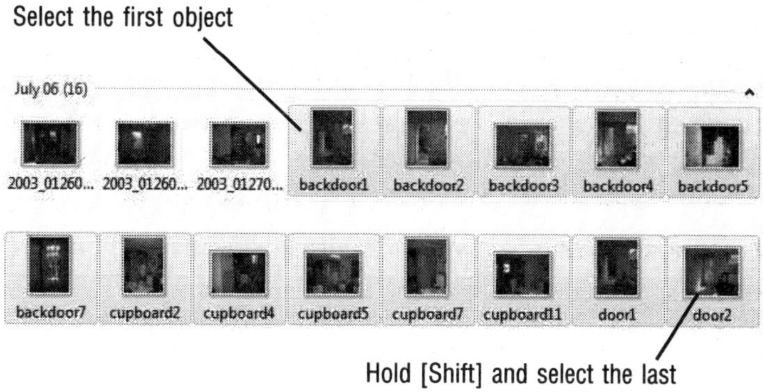

Select the first object

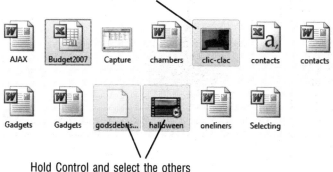

Hold [Shift] and select the last

Figure 4.3 Selecting a continuous group of icons in Explorer.

Scattered objects:

1 Highlight the first object.

2 Hold down [**Ctrl**] and highlight each object in turn.

3 If you select an object by mistake, point to (or click on) it again to remove the highlighting.

Select the first object

Hold Control and select the others

Figure 4.4 Selecting a scattered set of icons in Explorer.

4.2 Cut, Copy and Paste

If you look at the Edit menu of any Windows application, you will find the commands **Cut, Copy** and **Paste**. You will also find them on the short menu that opens when you right-click on a selected object. These are used for copying and moving data within and between applications.

*   **Copy** copies a selected block of text, picture, file or other object into a special part of memory called the *Clipboard*. Data stored in the Clipboard can be retrieved by any Windows application – not just the one that put it there.

*   **Cut** deletes selected data from the original application, but places a copy into the Clipboard.

*   **Paste** copies the data from the Clipboard into a different place in the same application, or into a different application – as long as this can handle data in that format.

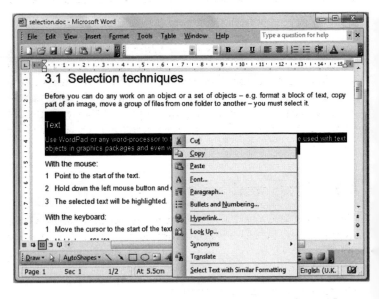

Figure 4.5 The right-click menu offers a quick route to the Cut and Paste commands. If the Clipboard is empty, Paste will be 'greyed out' or omitted from the menu.

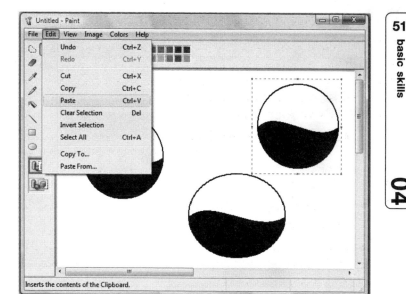

Figure 4.6 Pasting a copied image in Paint.

The data normally remains in the Clipboard until new data is copied or cut into it, or until Windows is shut down. (Some applications have a **Clear Clipboard** command.) If you want to see what's in the Clipboard – just for interest, as this serves few practical purposes – you can use the Clipboard Viewer. It should be on the **Programs ➔ Accessories ➔ Systems Tools** menu. (This is an optional utility and may not have been installed.)

4.3 Drag and drop

This is an alternative to Cut and Paste for moving objects within an application or between compatible applications. It is also the simplest way to rearrange files and folders, as you will see in the next chapter.

The technique is simple to explain:

1 Select the block of text or the object(s).

2 Point anywhere within the highlighted text or in the frame enclosing other objects.

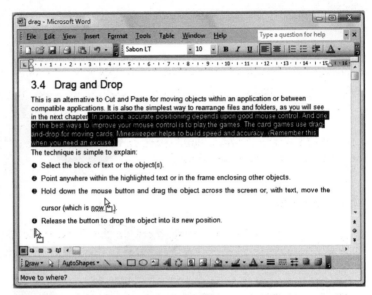

Figure 4.7 Dragging text in a word-processor (Word). The target position for the text is marked by the thin bar to the left of the arrow.

Figure 4.8 You can drag a file from Explorer and drop it into an application – this can be quicker than opening files from within the application.

3 Hold down the mouse button and drag the object across the screen or, with text, move the cursor (which is now 🖐).

4 Release the button to drop the object into its new position.

In practice, accurate positioning depends upon good mouse control. And one of the best ways to improve your mouse control is to play the games. The card games use drag-and-drop for moving cards; Minesweeper helps to build speed and accuracy. (Remember this when you need an excuse.)

4.4 Scraps

A 'scrap' is a special sort of file parked on the Desktop. It is typically a fragment of a word-processor document – though it could be the whole of one. Scraps can be used as highly visible reminders of urgent jobs, or to hold blocks of text that you will reuse in other files, or simply as temporary storage.

What distinguishes a scrap from an ordinary file are the ways that it is created and used.

1 Set the word-processor window into Restore mode so that some of the Desktop is visible.

2 Select the text.

3 Drag the selection and drop it on the Desktop.

4 To reuse the scrap, either drag it into the application window,

Or

5 Double-click on it to open the application and load in the scrap document.

Summary

- Text can be selected with the mouse or the keyboard.

- Graphics and other objects are selected by dragging an outline around them, or by using the mouse in conjunction with [Shift] or [Ctrl].

- Selected data can be cut or copied to the Clipboard, then pasted into the same or a different application.

- Text and some objects can be moved by drag and drop.

- Text can be stored on the Desktop as scraps.

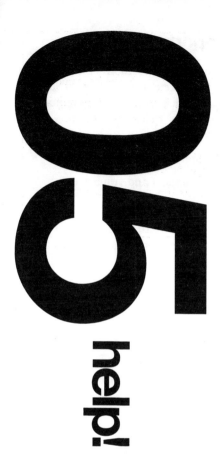

05

help!

In this chapter you will learn:

- about Help and Support
- how to browse and to search for the Help you need
- about troubleshooters
- how to get Help online
- about Help in applications

5.1 Help and Support

If you ever get stuck while using Windows, there's plenty of help at hand. Windows Vista has its own extensive Help and Support system with 'tours', 'tutorials' and interactive troubleshooters, and every Windows application has a Help system.

The main Windows Vista Help system is reached through the **Help and Support** item on the **Start** menu.

• Click **Start**, select **Help and Support** and you are in.

There are three sections in the opening page:

• **Find an answer** has six icons – five that lead to the built-in Help system in different ways, and one that takes you to the online Help at Microsoft.

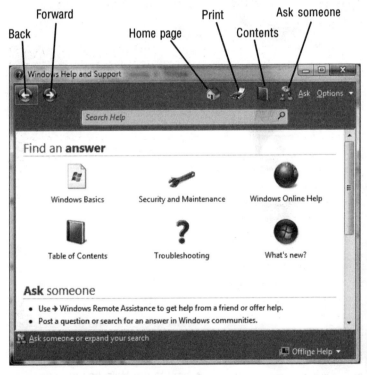

Figure 5.1 The Home page of the Help and Support system – the buttons at the top give quick access to the main tools, and notice the Search field.

- **Ask someone** gives you three ways to approach other people – friends and colleagues through Remote Assistance, other enthusiasts online through Windows Communities, and staff at Microsoft Customer Support.

- **Information from Microsoft** lists the pages that you have previously downloaded from the online Help – these are stored in case you need to refer to them again.

Windows Basics

This leads to a set of links, each leading to an article on a basic concept and/or technique. Within the articles you will then find other links taking you off to explore ideas in more detail, or demonstrating how things work.

1 Click the icon or the text for **Windows Basics**.

2 Click on a topic heading.

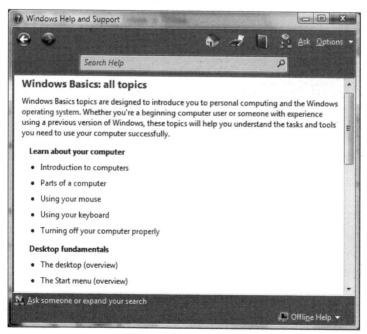

Figure 5.2 The Windows Basics area of the Help system – if you are new to Windows, you should at least dip into here early on.

3 The article will be displayed. Read it straight through, or…

4 Click a link in the **In this article** set on the right to jump down to a subtopic.

5 Click on any text in green to display a brief explanation of the term.

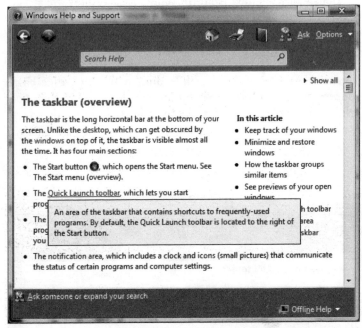

Figure 5.3 If text is in green clicking on it displays a tip. Notice ▸ Show all at the top right – click this to display any hidden details anywhere in the article. (See also step 7.)

6 Text in blue is usually a link to another article in the Help system. If the text has an ➔ arrow at the start, it tells you that clicking on the text will start a program, or open a dialog box, or do something similar. The Help article will stay open, so that you can read through its instructions while you try out the program, or whatever.

To add an e–mail account in Windows Mail

1. ➔ Click to open Windows Mail.

7 If you see blue text with an ▶ arrowhead to its left, this indicates there is more detail available under the header text. Click anywhere on the text to show the details.

8 When you have finished with an article, click ⬅ the Back button go back to the previous page – you may need to click ⬅ several times to reach the Home page again.

5.2 Table of Contents

This gives you access to the entire offline (built-in) Help system. It is arranged into 16 main areas, which are subdivided into subtopics – which may also be subdivided.

1 Click the **Table of Contents** icon or the text, or click ⬛ the toolbar button.

2 Click ⬛ beside a heading to open its folder. You will see a list

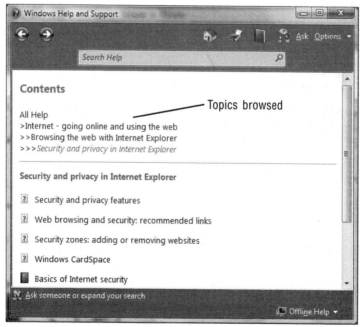

Figure 5.4 Browsing through the Contents. Note the list of topic headings at the top. These show the route you have taken to reach this page – click on any of these to jump back to that point in the system.

of articles and headings for subtopics – there can be anything from 0 to 10 or more articles and subtopics.

3 Click ■ to go to the next level of topics, if necessary.

4 Click ? to display an article.

5 Read, and follow up links until you find what you need. If you want to go back, click ◐ or click a heading in the list of topics through which you have browsed to reach this page.

♦ **Security and Maintenance** and **What's New?** are introductory articles, with selected links branching off from them. You can find them in the Contents, but they have been brought up to the Home page because they are important.

Troubleshooting

There are a limited number of troubleshooters, but they cover some of the more common problems. They can be very useful,

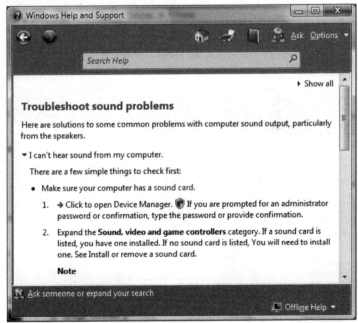

Figure 5.5 Troubleshooters often ask you to run a system tool – in this case Device Manager – to check settings and correct them if necessary.

especially when you are having difficulties with printers or other peripherals, or when you are trying to configure your Internet and e-mail software. They will normally take you through a series of checks to diagnose problems and can often tell you what to do to cure them.

1 Click the icon or the text for **Troubleshooting**.

2 Select the type of problem. You may be offered several alternatives at the next level.

3 Read through, clicking the ▶ icon to show detailed instructions, as necessary, to see if you can identify the problem.

Windows Online Help

This is organized in much the same way as the offline Help – the built-in system – but has two advantages: there is more in it, and it is regularly updated.

1 Click the icon or the text for **Windows Online Help**.

2 In the Find answers area, select a category, then pick a topic.

Figure 5.6 There's lots more Help available online.

Or

3 Click **Ask someone**. This will take you to Windows Vista Newsgroups. These can be good resources, particularly for more experienced users, but even new users may get some help here. At the top of the newsgroup page is a **Search For** box. Type one or more keywords to describe your problem and press [**Enter**]. After a few moments – this system is slow – you will get a list of messages that match your search. Browse through them. They are grouped into 'threads', with the first often being a request for help, and the later ones suggested solutions.

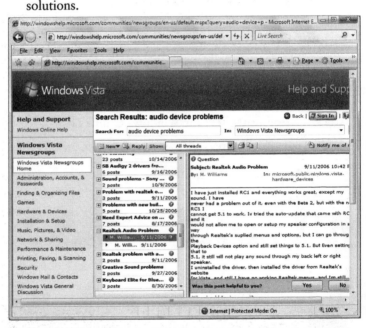

Figure 5.7 Browsing for help in the Vista newsgroups. If you want to ask questions, you must join – it's free and painless to do so!

Keywords

When searching in the newsgroups, or in the main Help system, a 'keyword' is simply a word that describes what you are looking for. If a word does not give you what you want, try a different word.

Search

The **Search** box is present in the toolbar on every page of the Help system. To run a search:

1 Type one or more keywords into the box and click 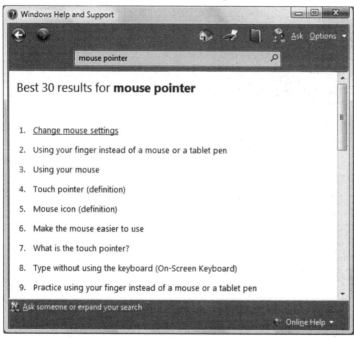.

2 The 'best' 30 results, i.e. those which Vista calculates will best match your search, will be listed. Click on a heading to display the page.

3 If you don't find what you want, try different keywords. Sometimes it is better to not be too specific.

Figure 5.8 Searching for Help. If Online Help is switched on at the time (see page 65), the routine will search the online Help system at Microsoft as well as the pages in your PC.

Search in applications

Many Windows programs have a Search box in the toolbar. Use this to find Help for that program.

5.3 Help tools and options

On the right of the toolbar there are five buttons:

- **Home** takes you back to the page you see when you first open Help and Support.

- **Print...** prints the current article.

- **Browse Help** takes you to the Table of Contents.

- **Ask** opens a page with links to get help online. You can use **Remote Assistance** to link your PC to a friend's so that you can see each other's screens and try to sort out the problem between you. You can also access the newsgroup **communities**, contact Customer Support online, search through the databases online, or phone Customer Services.

- **Options** repeats two of these tools, and gives you three more. Let's have a closer look at this.

Figure 5.9 The Help tools and options.

Options

There are five options:

- **Print...** and **Browse Help** are the same as the buttons.

- **Text Size** lets you adjust the size of the text.

- **Find (on this page)...** opens a dialog box where you can type in a word to search for on the current page only. This can be useful as some pages are rather long.

- **Settings...** controls the access to the online Help. This is also present on the Online/Offline Help button – which we are about to look at.

5.4 Offline and online Help

If you set up your system to get online Help, it will include the online Help and Support system when you run a search. If you have an always-on broadband connection to the Internet, this will normally be the best choice, because it will give you access to more and better Help. With a dial-up connection, it is generally better to only access online Help when you cannot find what you want offline.

To change the setting:

1 Click the Offline Help (or Online Help) button.

2 Select **Get online/offline Help** to change the setting for the current session.

Or

3 Select **Settings**.

4 Tick (or clear) the **Include Windows Online...** option.

5 Click **OK**.

Figure 5.10 This setting controls how the Help system normally works – you can override it during a session if you need to go online (or stay off).

5.5 Application Help

The utilities and applications that are supplied as part of Windows Vista have Help systems which follow the same pattern as the main Help and Support system. It's the same window and the links, Search facility and other routines are exactly the same, though the initial page and the way into the system do vary.

1 If there is a menu bar, look for **Help** on the far right. You will normally use the first item on this menu, which will be called **Help Topics** or **Contents** or something similar.

2 If there is no menu bar, look for a 🔘 icon and click that.

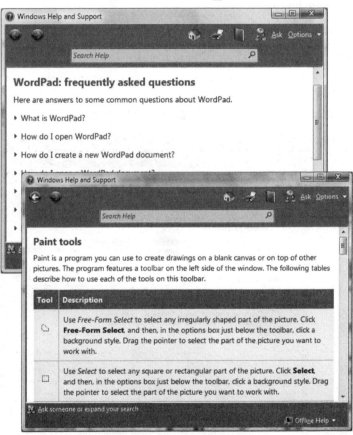

Figure 5.11 The initial Help pages for WordPad (top) and Paint (bottom).

Non-Vista Help systems

Other applications from Microsoft or other software producers also have their own Help systems. These vary in style and presentation, but normally behave in much the same way.

Contents

A Help system can be thought of as a book, with a different topic on every page – though, unlike paper books, the pages vary in length. Related topics are arranged into chapters, and the whole book is extensively indexed. But this is a reference book. Don't attempt to read it all from start to finish, you'll just give yourself a headache.

Help systems normally open at the **Contents** tab – if another tab is at the front, click on the **Contents** label to switch to it. Use this tab to get an overview of the available Help, and when you want to read around a topic. Initially, only the main section names will be visible.

Open a section → Revisit pages opened earlier

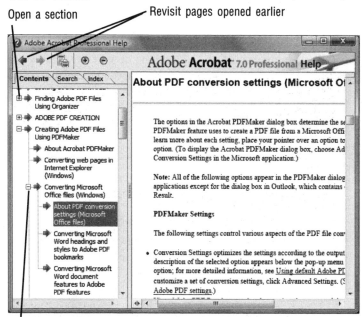

Close the section

Figure 5.12 The Help system of a non-Vista application.

♦ Beside each section name is a ⊞ icon. Click on the section name or the icon to open the section.

♦ Some sections have subsections. Again, click on the name or ⊞ to open one.

♦ When you see a list of topic pages, click on the name to display a page in the right-hand panel of the window.

♦ You can usually only open one section at a time – the open one will close when you select another. If you want to close a section, click the ⊟ icon.

♦ As you browse through the system, the **Back** and **Forwards** buttons become active, allowing you to return to pages that you have opened earlier in that session.

You can navigate around an application Help system, as you can in Vista Help and Support, following links, and moving backwards and forwards.

Index

You will find a Search facility in non-Vista Help systems, and it will work in just the same way as in Vista Help and Support. You will also find a third way of tracking down Help, that is not present in Vista. A Help **Index** works like the index in a book, with keywords listed in alphabetical order.

1 Start to type a keyword into the box at the top. The list will scroll to bring into view words that start with those letters.

2 If the word you want is not yet visible, type more letters.

3 If an entry has ⊞ to the side, it has sub-entries. Click the icon to display them.

4 Select an entry to display the relevant page.

♦ In some systems, if an entry leads to several Help pages, you will see a **Topics Found** list – select one from here.

Creating the Index

The first time that you use the Index, you may have to wait while the system scans the Help pages to create it.

Type the first letter(s) of the word

Click to display sub-entries

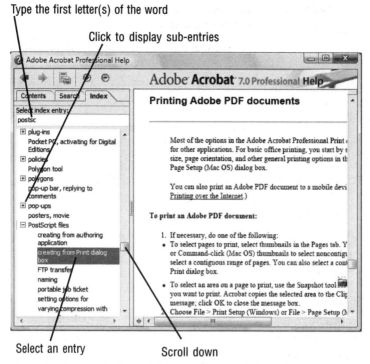

Select an entry   Scroll down

Figure 5.13 Using the **Index** tab in an application Help system.

5.6 Tips and prompts

Tooltips

The icons on tool buttons are generally good *reminders* of the nature of the tool, but they are not always immediately obvious to the new user. Tooltips are little pop-up labels that tell you what icons stand for.

Status bar prompts

The Status bar serves many purposes – it is through here that applications will communicate with you, so do keep an eye on it. In some applications it is used to display a brief description of items as you point to them in the menus.

Wait a moment for the Tooltip

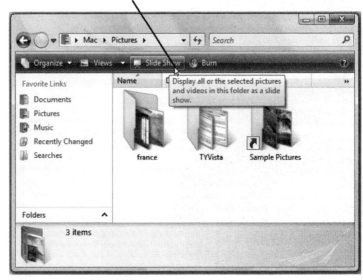

Figure 5.14 If you don't know what an icon does, point to it and wait a second. A Tooltip will appear, giving its name. If you still need Help with it, at least you now know what to look up in the Index.

Summary

+ You can get into Windows' Help and Support system from the option on the Start menu.

+ To browse through Help and Support, pick a topic from the headings on the Home page.

+ To find Help and Support on a specific topic run a Search.

+ Troubleshooters can be helpful in solving problems.

+ Additional Help is available online.

+ The Help systems in applications may look different from Vista Help and Support but are used in much the same way. Browse through the Contents or track down specific Help pages through the Index or Search tabs.

+ Tooltips and Status bar prompts can help you to get to grips with the tools and commands in a new application.

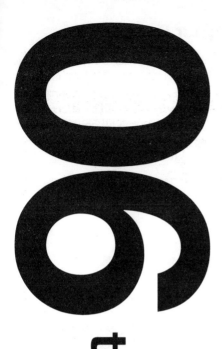

06

the desktop

In this chapter you will learn:

- how to personalize your Desktop
- how to change mouse pointers
- how to change the sounds
- about the Display settings
- about Desktop icons
- how to add gadgets to your Desktop and configure them

6.1 Personalize your Desktop

You can change the colour scheme, the background, the mouse pointers, the sounds and other aspects of your PC. You may not want to tackle all of them at one sitting, but that's not a problem. You can change any of the settings whenever and as often as you like. If the PC has several users, then they can all have their own Desktop settings which will be applied when they log on. Feel free to experiment – it's your Desktop.

1 Right-click anywhere on the background of the Desktop.

2 Select **Personalize** from the menu.

3 The **Personalize** window will open. The main panel holds links to seven routines for customizing the Desktop. Note also the links at the top and bottom of the sidebar on the left.

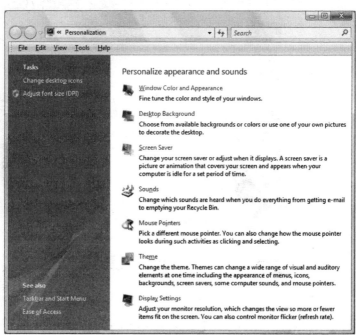

Figure 6.1 The Personalize window.

The instructions in the next few sections all assume that you have reached this point.

6.2 Color and Appearance

Use this panel to set the style, colour and fonts for the Desktop and standard Windows elements in all applications – the window frames, menus, dialog boxes, etc.

The initial display is concerned with colour and transparency. There are seven preset colours, but you can also mix your own.

1   Select **Window Color and Appearance**.

2   Pick a colour, or click **Show color mixer** and adjust the Hue, Saturation and Brightness levels to get the desired mix.

3   If you want transparent window frames, tick **Enable transparency** and drag the slider to set the level.

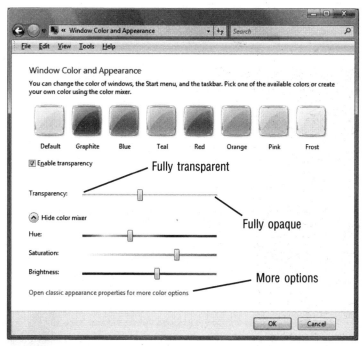

Figure 6.2 Setting the colours.

4 Click **Open classic appearance properties**. This opens the **Appearance Settings** dialog box. The only option here is **Color scheme** – and you might want to have a look at those, especially if a high contrast display would be useful to you – but there are also two important buttons.

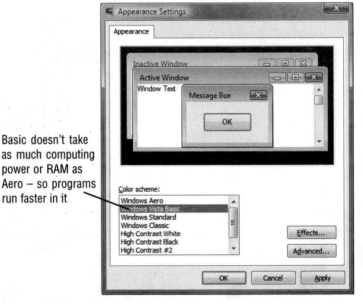

Basic doesn't take as much computing power or RAM as Aero – so programs run faster in it

Figure 6.3 The Appearance Settings dialog box.

5 Click **Effects**.

6 One of the options is **Show window contents while dragging**, which we met earlier (page 41). These are all purely decorative – turn them on or off as you choose, then click **OK**.

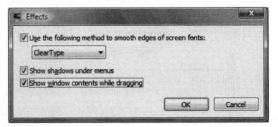

7 Click the **Advanced** button to open this dialog box where you can set the colour, font and size of individual elements.

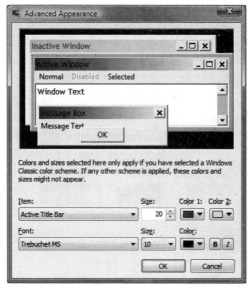

Figure 6.4 The Advanced Appearance dialog box.

8 Click on an item in the preview pane, or select it from the **Item** list, then set its size, colour and font as required.

9 Click **OK** to return to the **Properties** panel.

10 Click **OK** to return to the main **Personalize** window.

6.3 The Background

The background is purely decorative! The background can be a plain colour, a single picture or a small image 'tiled' to fill the whole screen. Windows Vista has a selection of small and large images, but any JPG, GIF or BMP image can be used.

1 Make sure that as much background as possible is visible before you start this – you will see why at Step 4.

2 Click the **Desktop Background** link.

3 Click the button by **Picture Locations** to get a list of available folders. (The **Browse** button will let you reach any folder in your system, but you might want to leave this until after you have learned about files and folders in the next chapter.)

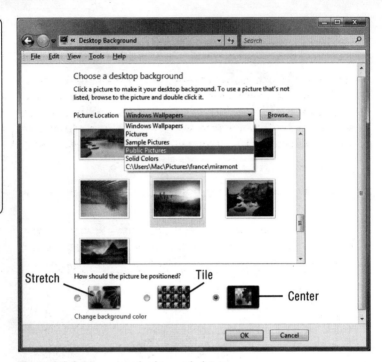

Figure 6.5 Setting a new background picture.

4 Scroll through the display of pictures and click on one if it catches your fancy. It will be applied to the background so that you can see how it looks. If you don't like it, try another. A picture will only be fixed in place if you click **OK**.

5 If the picture is smaller than the screen, use the position options at the bottom to either **Stretch** it to fill the screen, or **Tile** it across and down, or **Center** it in its natural size.

6 Click **OK** to fix the choice, or **Cancel** to revert to the current background.

6.4 The screen saver

This is mainly decorative. A screen saver is a moving image that takes over the screen if the computer is left unattended for a while. On older monitors this prevented a static image from burning a permanent ghost image into the screen. Newer monitors do not suffer from this, and in fact, most now have an energy saving feature that turns them off when they are not in use. If your monitor has this, the screen saver will only be visible briefly, if at all.

A screen saver can be password protected (or revert to the log-on screen if there are several users), so that it will lock your PC until the password is entered. This can be useful if you do not want passers-by to read your screen while you are away from your desk – it is like putting Lock on automatic, with a time delay.

1 In the **Personalize** window, select **Screen Saver**.

2 Pick a saver from the drop-down list – check the preview to see how it will look.

3 With some savers you can set the speed, colour, text or other features. Click the **Settings** button to see if there are options.

Figure 6.6 The Screen Saver dialog box. Click the Change power settings link to set the times that the system should wait before shutting down the monitor and the hard drive. Don't make these waits too short. Turning a monitor on and off constantly may well reduce its lifespan.

4 Set the Wait time – how long does the computer have to be idle before the screen saver should kick in?

5 If you want to protect your PC, tick the **On resume, display logon screen** checkbox.

6.5 Mouse pointers

These options are purely decorative, though anything which makes it easier to see what you are doing must be beneficial. There are a dozen or so pointers, each related to a different mouse action. You can pick a whole new scheme or change individual pointers.

1 In the **Personalize** window, select **Mouse Pointers**.

2 Drop down the **Scheme** list and select a scheme. The icons in the display will change to match.

3 To change an individual pointer, select it and click **Browse**. You can then pick a new one from the *Cursors* folder.

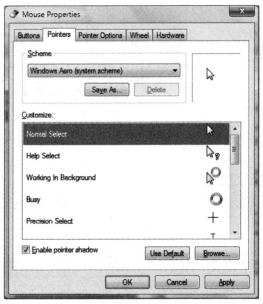

Figure 6.7 Changing the Mouse Pointers. If you have a customized set that you might want to reapply in future, click Save As... and save it. It will then be added to the Scheme list.

6.6 Sounds

Windows attaches sounds to certain events so that you get, for example, a fanfare at start up and a warning noise when you are about to do something you may later regret. Some of these are just for fun, others can be very useful. If you tend to watch the keyboard, rather than the screen, when you are typing, then an audible warning can help to alert you to a situation before it becomes a problem.

The **Sounds** link leads you to the **Sounds** tab of the **Sound** panel, where you can decide which events are to be accompanied by a sound, and which sounds to use. There are several schemes and a selection of individual sounds supplied with Windows, or you can use your own .wav files. (You can create these with Sound Recorder – explore it one day, it's simple to use.)

1 In the **Personalize** window, select **Sounds**.

2 If you want to change the overall style of your sounds, select a scheme from the list.

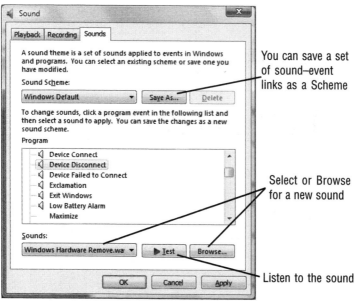

Figure 6.8 Selecting a new sound to attach to an event. If you want to turn off a sound, select 'None' in the Sounds list.

3 To change the sound assigned to an event, select the program event from the list then either pick a sound from the **Sounds** list, or click **Browse** and locate the file on your hard disk.

4 Click ▶ Test to hear the current sound.

5 When you have finished, click **OK**.

Or

6 Click **Save As...** if you want to save the scheme so that it can be reapplied later.

6.7 Display Settings

The Display Settings relate to the size of the screen and number of colours used in the display. They should normally be left at their defaults as Windows Vista will select the optimum settings for your system – and the Advanced settings should certainly be left alone unless you know and understand the details of your system. Bad selections here can really mess up your screen!

Figure 6.9 The Display Settings are generally best left at their defaults.

6.8 Desktop icons

Over on the top left of the Personalize window are two Tasks and the first of these is **Change Desktop Icons**. The icons are shortcuts to key programs and folders. Initially you may find that only the Recycle Bin (which you can use to recover deleted files) and Computer (which displays the disks and drives on the PC) may be present – it depends upon the installation.

Click on the checkboxes to toggle the display of the icons for Computer, Recycle Bin, User's Files (your own document folder), Internet Explorer, Network and the Control Panel. Turn off those that you do not use.

Note that you can select new images for some icons – select the icon, then click **Change Icon** and pick a different image.

There may not be many icons on your Desktop yet, but when you install applications, these will often add their own icons. And you can create your own shortcuts – we will come back to this in the next chapter.

Figure 6.10 Selecting the Desktop icons to display.

6.9 Gadgets

Gadgets are mini-applications that you can add to your Desktop. Some are handy utilities, some the latest news headlines, stock reports or weather forecasts from the Web, others are just for fun. All are worth exploring.

The gadgets are normally shown in the Sidebar, which sits on the right of the Desktop. If this is not visible, click the 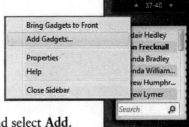 Sidebar icon in the Notification area.

Adding gadgets

There are around a dozen gadgets supplied as part of the Vista package, and more available online. These can be added at any time – and removed again if you find that you do not use them.

To add a gadget:

1   Right-click anywhere on the Sidebar.

2   Select **Add Gadgets...**

3   At the gadgets window, right-click on a gadget and select **Add**.

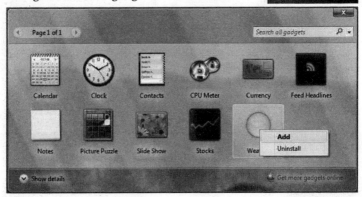

Figure 6.11 Adding a gadget.

Gadgets can be customized and/or controlled, but in different ways, depending upon what they are.

They all have a mini-toolbar which appears when you point to the top right. It has three parts: a Close button, an Options button and a Handle which is used for moving it.

The Clock

With the clock, you can change the face, name and the time zone. (You can have several clocks, each set to a different time zone, in which case the name could identify the location.)

1 Point to the top right to get the toolbar and click the **Options** button – the Clock options dialog box will appear.

2 Use the arrows to cycle through the choice of faces until you find the one you prefer.

3 If you have several clocks, type in a name to suit the location.

4 Select a time zone.

5 Tick the **Show the second hand** box, if it is wanted.

6 Click **OK**.

Figure 6.12 Setting the options for the Clock.

The Calendar

This can show the day's date or the whole month. It has no options, but responds to clicks.

In month mode:

1 Click on the arrows at the top left and right to switch to previous and later months.

2 Click on any day to display that day only.

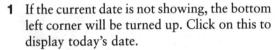

In day mode:

1 If the current date is not showing, the bottom left corner will be turned up. Click on this to display today's date.

2 Click anywhere else on the calendar to switch to month mode.

Contacts

This displays the people in your Contacts list (see page 212), and holds their e-mail address and phone number, so that you can contact them directly from here. Here's how:

1 Use the slider to scroll through the list to find the person you want to contact.

Or

2 Type some or all of the name in the Search box.

3 Click on the name to select. The person's card will be pulled to the front.

4 Click on the e-mail address to start to send them a message. The New Message window in Windows Mail will open ready for you to start typing. (See Chapter 13.)

5 Click on the top, red, tab on the left of the gadget to display the full list again.

Feed headlines

Feeds are brief notices sent out by websites to alert you to new material as it appears on the site. You can set the gadget to one (or all) of four feeds from Microsoft, and these offer differing mixtures of news and tips.

To set up the feeds:

1 Point to a spot to the top right of the gadget, and click on the tiny magnifying glass.

2 Select the feed to displays, and the number to show.

3 Click **OK**.

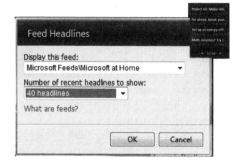

To read feeds:

1 Use the up and down arrows at the bottom to scroll through the headlines.

2 Click on a headline to display a summary of the story.

3 Click on the summary title if you want to read the full story online. It will pass the link to the browser and download the story from the Web.

Go to
the Web

Scroll control

Figure 6.13 Reading Feed stories.

Notes

Need somewhere to write your shopping lists and reminders? Add this gadget to the Sidebar and you can write yourself a note whenever you need one. It couldn't be simpler to use, and the options are likewise straightforward – you can change the colour, font and size.

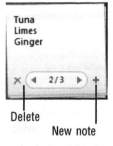

Delete

New note

Slide Show

This is purely decorative. It will cycle through the images in any chosen folder, showing each one for a set length of time.

If you want a closer look at a picture, there's a View tool that will open it in the Photo Gallery (see page 235) – point to anywhere on the gadget to make the toolbar appear.

View

The folder, display time and transition between pictures are set in the options dialog box.

Picture Puzzle

This is a sliding block puzzle, and can consume hours of time if you are not careful – it's not as easy at you might think!

Click on any block adjacent to the space to move that block into it.

The options dialog box offers a dozen images to pick from.

6.10 Gadget controls

These apply to all gadgets. Right-click on a gadget to display its menu of controls.

There are only half a dozen. **Add Gadgets, Options** and **Close Gadget** are obvious. The rest are worth a closer look.

* **Detach from Sidebar** – when a gadget is detached, it initially goes to the top left of the Desktop, though it can be dragged from there to anywhere on screen. Some gadgets become larger when detached – Calendar shows the month *and* the day, Slide Show, Feed Headlines and other information displays become twice the size.

* **Move** – selects the gadget so that you can move it within the Sidebar. To move it, you need to drag on the handle.

   Note: you can drag on the handle without using Move, and that you can drag it off the Sidebar, detaching it, if you like.

* **Opacity** – the gadgets can be distracting. If you reduce their opacity and make them more transparent, they are less eye catching. When you point to one, it becomes solid once more.

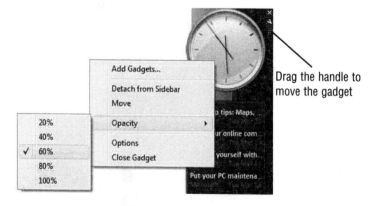

Figure 6.14 Setting the Opacity level.

Summary

- ◆ You can personalize your Desktop to suit yourself.

- ◆ The Color and Appearance options set the colour and transparency of the display.

- ◆ The Background and Screen Saver options are largely decorative and have little impact on the working of your system.

- ◆ There are several sets of mouse pointers that you can choose from.

- ◆ You can change the sounds attached to events.

- ◆ The Display Settings are normally best left at their defaults.

- ◆ There are half a dozen standard icons which you can display on your Desktop if you use them.

- ◆ You can fill your Desktop with gadgets – and some of them may even be useful!

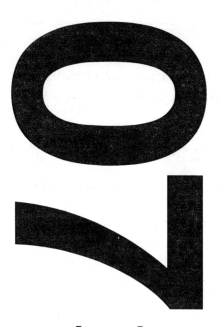

07 files and folders

In this chapter you will learn:

- about folders and file storage
- how to use and customize Windows Explorer
- about file associations
- how to manage files
- about the Recycle Bin
- how to search for files

7.1 Disks and folders

To be able to use your computer efficiently, you must know how to manage your files – how to find, copy, move, rename and delete them – and how to organize the folders on your disks. In Vista, these jobs are done through Windows Explorer. In this chapter we will have a look at this vital program and see how it is used for file and folder management. We will also look at creating links between documents and applications, and at the Recycle Bin – a neat device which makes it much less likely that you will delete files by accident.

A floppy disk holds 1.4MB of data – enough for a few decent-sized documents or a couple of pictures. A typical hard drive holds 80 Gigabytes – nearly 50,000 times as much! Obviously, with this much storage space, it must be organized if you are ever to find anything. The organization comes through *folders*. A folder is an elastic-sided division of the disk. It can contain any number of files and subfolders – which can contain other subfolders, and so on ad infinitum. The structure is sometimes described as a tree. The *root* is at the drive level. The main folders branch off from here, and each may have a complex set of branches leading from it. At the simplest, a C: drive might contain three folders – *Program Files* (with subfolders for each application), *Users* (with subfolders for each user) and *Windows* (which has subfolders for the sets of programs and files that make up the Windows Vista system). You can create new folders, and rename, delete or move them to produce your own structure.

7.2 Windows Explorer

Unlike every other Windows application, Windows Explorer (or Explorer for short) does not have its name in the title bar, and it is rarely started by name. We noted earlier that documents are associated with applications, which will start when you open the document. In exactly the same way, Explorer is associated with folders and the normal way of starting it is to open a folder.

♦ Open the **Start** menu and click **Computer**. This will run Explorer and open the *Computer* folder, which holds all the disk drives on your system.

Current folder   Toolbar   Search box

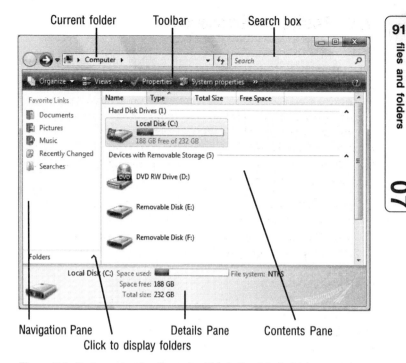

Navigation Pane   Details Pane   Contents Pane
Click to display folders

Figure 7.1 Explorer showing Computer. This is the default display.

The Explorer display is highly variable. Some elements can be turned on or off, and some change in response to the material that is currently displayed. These are always present:

* The **Current Folder** box shows you where you are now.

* The **Search** box can be used to hunt for a file (see page 118).

* The **Toolbar** buttons vary according to what sort of folder is displayed, and what sort of file, if any, is selected at the time.

* The **Contents Pane** usually shows the files and folders in the current folder, though for *Computer* it shows the disks and other storage on the PC.

These are optional, though the first two are normally present.

* The **Navigation Pane** has two parts: **Favorite Links** lets you open your most-used folders with one click; **Folders** shows the structure of folders – and we'll come back to this shortly.

- The **Details Pane** tells you the size, date and other details about the selected file or folder.

- The **Preview Pane** shows a small version of an image or the first page of other documents, if a preview is available.

- The **Search Pane** opens up when you run an advanced search (see page 118).

- The **Menu Bar** gives another way to reach the commands and options. Compared to the selected and context-sensitive Toolbar, which changes as you work, this has the advantage that every command is always there, and in the same place.

To turn the optional panes and Menu Bar on or off:

1 Click on the **Organize** button. Point to **Layout** and click on an element to toggle its display.

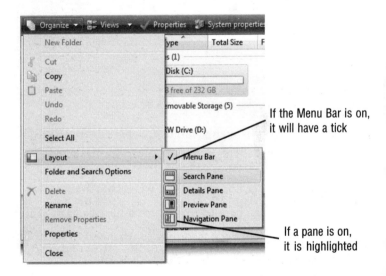

If the Menu Bar is on, it will have a tick

If a pane is on, it is highlighted

2 If you turn on the Preview Pane in *Computer*, there will be nothing to see. Let's find something. Click *Documents* in the **Favorite Links** list.

3 Check that the Preview Pane is present – it may not be, as Explorer opens each folder with the same display as was used previously. Turn it on if necessary.

Back – return to the last folder you viewed

Menu Bar

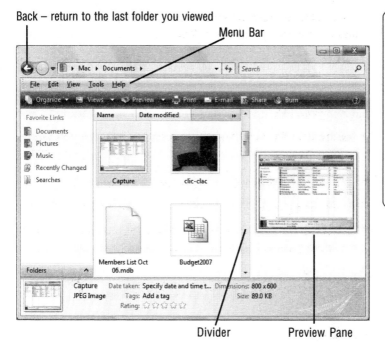

Divider   Preview Pane

Figure 7.2 If the window is too small the Preview Pane cannot be opened.

4 Select a file and see if it has a preview.

5 The preview will be scaled to fit the Preview Pane. If you want to change the size of the pane, drag on the divider.

7.3 View options

Files and folders can be shown as **Icons**, ranging in size from **Small** to **Extra Large, List, Details** or **Tiles**. The display is controlled through the **Views** button on the toolbar.

The **Icons** views show – if possible – an image of each file, and otherwise an icon to identify its type. They work best, of course, with images, but documents with previews can also be displayed. Make the icons as large as you need to be able to identify files.

Small Icons and **List** differ mainly in the order of the icons – **Icons** lists across the screen and leaves more space between them. Both are good for selecting sets of files.

Details gives a column display of *properties* under the headings Name, Type, Size, Tags, Date modified and others (these vary – see *Choose Details* below). Every file has properties. Some of these are set by the system, e.g. its type, size, date modified, and others can be changed by you, e.g. its name and where it is stored. Some properties are common to all types of files, but some types have additional properties that hold further information.

Tiles displays for each file a large icon (so it is easy to identify the type), plus details of its type and size.

To change the view:

1 Click the **Views** button to cycle between the main types.

Or

2 Click the arrow beside the Views button to see the options.

3 Click on a name to select a view.

Or

4 Drag the slider to adjust the size – you can stop part-way between two set views to get an intermediate size.

Click to change   Drag to adjust

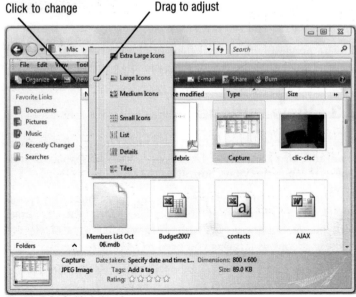

Figure 7.3 Setting the view.

View menu options

If you turn on the Menu Bar, you will have some additional layout and view options. Two are well worth knowing about.

Status Bar

If it has been turned on, the **Status Bar** lies at the bottom of the window and shows the number of objects in the folder and the amount of memory they use, or the size of a selected file.

• Open the **View** menu and tick **Status Bar** to turn it on.

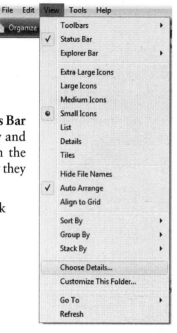

Choose Details

You can choose which properties to include in the headings. This determines the properties that are displayed in Details view, but also affects the way that you can sort and group files in any view – see section 7.6, *Sorting and grouping files*.

1 Right-click anywhere along the headings. The menu lists the more important properties.

2 Click on a property name to toggle the tick on or off.

3 If you can't see the property you want to include, click **More...**

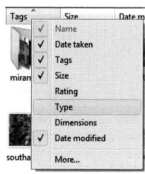

4   At the **Choose Details** dialog box, tick the details you want to include.

5   The order of the columns in the display matches the order in this list. Select a detail and use the **Move Up** and **Move Down** buttons to rearrange its order if required.

6   Click **OK**.

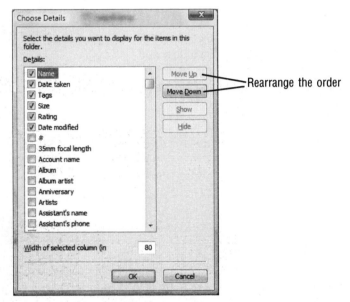

Rearrange the order

Figure 7.4 Different types of files have different details which can be displayed.

7.4 Folders

At the bottom of the Navigation Pane, you will see a bar labelled Folders, with an up arrow on the right.

Click on this to open up the Folders display. This gives you easier ways to switch between folders, and to move files between them. It shows the disk drives, folders and network connections in a branching structure.

- A ▷ icon to the left of a folder name shows that the folder has subfolders. Click this to open up the branch. The icon changes to ◢ and clicking this will close the branch.

When a folder is selected, its files and subfolders are listed in the main pane.

Top-level folders   Click to close the Folders display

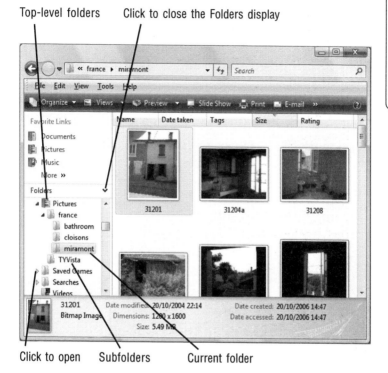

Click to open   Subfolders   Current folder

Figure 7.5 Navigating through the folders.

Organizing folders

Windows Vista sets up three folders for your files, *Documents*, *Pictures* and *Music*. These are unlikely to be enough for very long. You may need to create folders if:

- you will be storing more than a few dozen documents – it's hard to find stuff in crowded folders;

- your documents fall into distinct categories – personal, hobbies, different areas of work, etc.

It doesn't matter if you put documents of different types in the same folder. It might look untidy when you view it in Explorer – though sorting by Type will help to clarify. In practice, you mainly access your documents through applications, and when you open a file there, the **Open File** dialog boxes will normally only list those of the right type.

Creating folders

A new folder can be created at any time, and at any point in the folder structure. Here's how:

1 In Explorer, select the folder which will contain the new one, or select the drive letter for a new top-level folder.

2 Open the **File** menu, point to **New** and select **Folder**.

The new folder will be inside Pictures

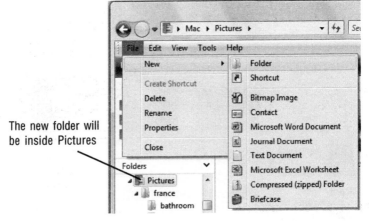

Or

3 Click the **Organize** button and select **New Folder**.

4 Replace *New Folder* with a meaningful name.

• If you decide the folder is in the wrong place, select it and drag it into place in the Folders list.

> ### Folders are files
>
> We think of folders as containers, but to the PC they are files, with lists of the names and disk locations of other files. They are special – you cannot read them – but they can be renamed, copied and deleted the same as document files.

Shortcuts to folders

A Desktop shortcut offers a simple and quick way to open a folder – as long as you can see the Desktop! You can create new shortcuts in several ways. This is probably the easiest.

1 Select the folder in Explorer.

2 Hold down the right mouse button and drag the icon onto the Desktop. The label **Move to Desktop** will appear beside it. This is the default action, but if you are holding down the right mouse button, you have some options.

3 Release the button and a menu will appear. Select **Create Shortcuts Here**.

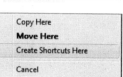

4 Click the icon to open the folder in Explorer.

Navigation buttons

At the top left of the Explorer window are three buttons which you can use to go back to folders that you have already been in during the session. You can:

♦ Go back to the last folder.

♦ Go forward again, after going back.

♦ Select a folder from the drop-down list.

Back
Forward
Open list

7.5 Tags

Tags are a type of property that can be used to sort, filter and group files in Explorer displays. They give you a more flexible way of organizing files – I have found tags handy for classifying digital photos, but they can help in any situation where a file could fit into several categories.

Not all types of files can take tags. For example, you can add them to Word documents, other Microsoft Office files and JPGs (the standard digital photo format) but not to text files, BMP images or Web pages.

1 Make sure that the Details Pane is present in Explorer.

2 Select the document.

Figure 7.6 Starting to add a tag to a JPG image.

3 In the Details Pane, click where it says **Tags:** *Add a tag* – and if it doesn't say it, you can't add any.

4 If this is the first time you have used the tag, type it in.

5 To add another tag, type a semicolon (;). *Add a tag* will reappear, and you are back to step 4.

6 Tags are stored by the system. If you want to add a tag that you have already used for other files, type the first letter or two. Any that contain the same letters will

Tags: j
Rating:
☐ July 05
☐ July 06
☐ june 05

be listed below the Tags box – click one to select. It will be written in for you and "; *Add a tag*" dropped in at the end, ready for the next.

7 Click back into the main display, or anywhere out of the Tags box to end.

• If you want to remove a tag at any point, select the file and click into the **Tags** box in the Details Pane.

Editing tags

You cannot edit a tag once you have added it. If you decide it is not right, you must delete it and type a new one.

7.6 Sorting and grouping files

Sorting

The simplest way to sort files into order is to click on a heading. This will arrange them in ascending order by that property – and it works in any view, not just Details, where the properties are visible. Click a second time to arrange them in descending order. This can be useful for tracking down files that you were working on at a certain date (but have forgotten the names), or for finding old or large files if you need to create some space.

Group

In this new Vista version, Explorer allows you to display files in groups. The groups can be based on any property that is present in the headings, so you can pull together files by type, or find those created during a given period, or group by tags. Tags have a unique effect on groups – if a file has more that one tag, it will be included in every matching group. This can produce a huge

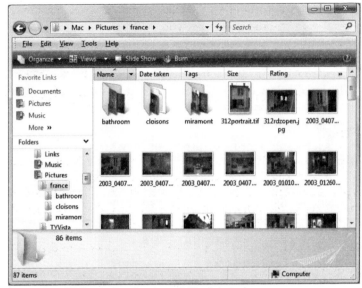

Figure 7.7 Click on a heading to sort files into order.

Group name

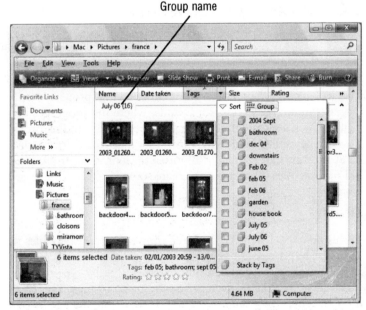

Figure 7.8 Files arranged by group – in this case, based on tags.

increase in the number of items on display, but the grouping makes it simpler to find the ones you want.

1 Click the down arrow on the property you want to use.

2 Click the **Group** button at the top of the drop-down menu.

3 Scroll through, checking the name on the dividing lines.

Filter

When you drop down the menu from a property heading, you will see the way the files can be grouped – a list of tags or file types, alphabetical or size ranges, or whatever is appropriate to the property. You can use these same criteria to filter the display, so that only those from selected groups are shown.

1 Click the down arrow on the property you want to use.

2 Tick those groups that you want to include – the display will change to show the selected ones and hide the rest.

3 Click the **Group** button if you want the group headers.

4 Click anywhere off the menu to close it.

Figure 7.9 Selecting groups of files to include.

Group/filter by name or size

Obviously names are unique, so you can't use them for grouping – instead files are grouped by alphabetical ranges. In the same way, size ranges are used for grouping.

Clearing a filter

To restore the display so that all the files are included, you can either tick every box in the list or clear the ticks from them all – do which ever takes fewest clicks!

Filter by date

Filtering by date is different from filtering by other properties in that *you* can specify the date range. In all the rest the filters are based on groups, and the ranges – if any – are set by Vista.

1 Click the down arrow on the **Date taken/modified** heading.

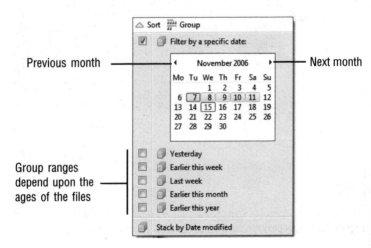

Previous month

Next month

Group ranges depend upon the ages of the files

2 To change the month, use the arrows either side of the month name to move backwards and forwards.

3 If you need to change the year, click on the Month–Year label and use the similar arrows there to move to another year. Click on the month name to display its days.

4 Click on a day to select it.

Or

5 Click on the first day, then hold down **[Shift]** and click on the last day to include.

6 Click anywhere on the main display to close the menu.

Stack

This is a variation on grouping. The stack routine arranges files into 'virtual folders', and you have to open these to see the files.

1 Click the down arrow on the property you want to use.

2 If you want to filter the groups, tick the ones to include.

3 Click the **Stack by** button at the bottom of the menu.

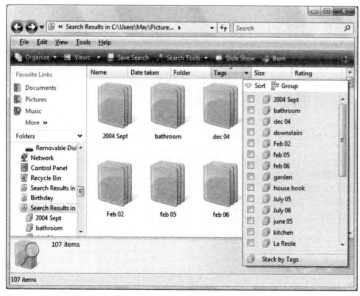

Figure 7.10 Stacking files – note the Search results in the Folders list.

4 Click on a folder to see its contents.

Notice that these virtual folders are stored by Vista as search results, and are added to the Folders list below the real folders and drives. They will remain here until you close Explorer.

7.7 Folder types and options

Windows Vista has default settings for five different types of folders – those that hold documents, pictures and videos, music details, music icons or all types. If you set a folder to the type appropriate to its contents, it will help you to get the best display.

1 Right-click on a folder in the Contents Pane or Folder list and select **Properties**.

2 At the **Properties** dialog box, switch to the **Customize** tab.

3 Drop down the folder type list and select the most suitable.

With some folder types you will see a **Choose File...** button which lets you choose an image to show on the folder icon

There may be a **Change Icon...** option that will let you pick the icon for the folder

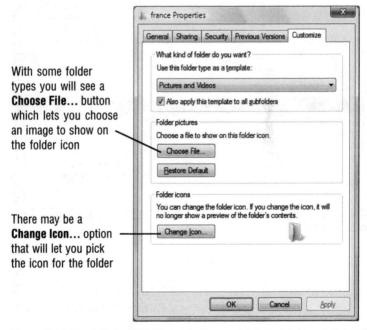

Figure 7.11 Check that a folder is set to the most appropriate type before looking at the folder options.

Folder Options

Folder Options are crucial to how you view and manage your files and folders. To reach it, open the **Tools** menu and select **Folder Options,** or click the **Organize** button and select **Folder and Search Options.**

General options

On the **General** tab under **Tasks,** select **Show preview and filters** for the Vista experience, or **Use Windows classic folders** for a simpler file display.

In the **Browse Folders** option, opening each folder in its own window is useful for moving files from one to another, but can produce a cluttered screen.

The **Click items as follows** settings apply to all files and folders, whether on the Desktop or in Windows Explorer.

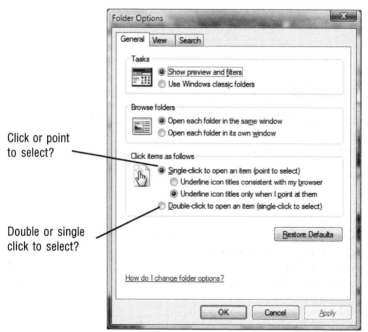

Click or point to select?

Double or single click to select?

Figure 7.12 The General tab of Folder Options.

View options

Some of the options here really are just fine-tuning, and you can come back and play with these when you want to see what they do. The more significant ones are covered here.

Most of the **Advanced Settings** should be left at their defaults until you have been using Windows for a while. A couple are worth checking now.

Hidden files – Windows Vista 'hides' essential files, to prevent accidental deletion. They can be shown if you want to see them, or these and system files – also crucial – can be hidden. For safety, hide them.

Remember each folder's view settings will retain the separate options from one session to the next. The settings can be different for each folder – which makes sense. You may well want more detail in folders that contain documents than in those that contain program or system files.

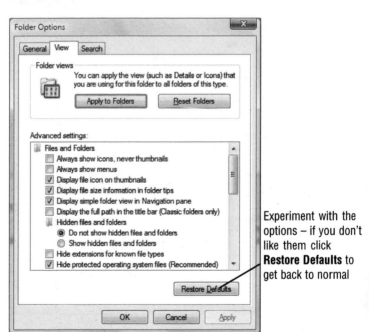

Experiment with the options – if you don't like them click **Restore Defaults** to get back to normal

Figure 7.13 The View tab of Folder Options.

Click **Apply to Folders** if you want the current settings – principally the choice of **View** – to be applied to all folders of this type. If you have got into a bit of a mess with your options (easily done!), click **Reset Folders** to go back to the original settings.

Search options

Here you can specify what, how and when to search. Windows creates indexes for the documents that you create, and these store the author, tags, and other properties. The default search routine looks through these indexes, and through the names of other non-indexed files (mainly those of application and system programs).

In the **What to search** section, you can extend a search so that it also looks through the text of documents – very thorough, but rather slow, or restrict it to filenames – faster but you have to know some or all of the name.

In the **How to search** section the key option is probably **Find partial matches**. If this is on, the search can find files based on a

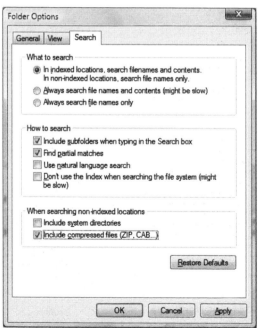

Figure 7.14 Setting the search options.

few letters of a name or tag. The catch is, that it may find far too many that match those few letters.

Under **When searching non-indexed location**, you would not normally want to search the system folders, but if you have stored documents in compressed folders, to save space, you may well want to search them.

7.8 File associations

Documents are associated with applications, so that picking a document from a folder or from the **Recent Items** list on the **Start** menu will start up its application and open the document within it. But many types of documents can be opened by several different applications. The question is, which one to use? When applications are installed, the system records which types of files they can handle. It will normally make one program the default for each type of document. You can set a default program if there is not yet one in place, and you can change the existing defaults.

The simplest way to set or change default programs is to do it as needed, one file type at a time, from within Windows Explorer.

1 Right-click on a document in the Contents Pane.

2 Point to **Open With** and select **Choose Default Program...**

Edit	
Print	
Preview	
🎨 Windows Photo Gallery	Open With ▶
🖌 Paint	
📄 Windows Wordpad Application	Share...
🖼 Microsoft Office Picture Manager	Restore previous versions
Choose Default Program...	Send To ▶
	Cut
	Copy
	Create Shortcut
	Delete
	Rename
	Properties

3 The recommended programs – the ones Windows knows about – will be listed at the top. It may be possible to use others, but it's safest not to. Select the one to use.

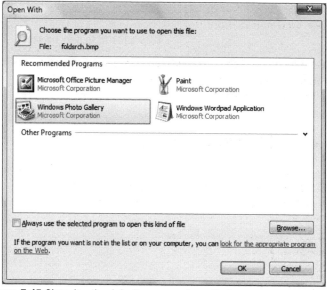

Figure 7.15 Choosing the default program for a file type.

4   Tick **Always use the selected program** to set it as the default.

5   Click **OK**.

7.9   File management

As a general rule, application files should be left well alone. Mess with these and your programs may not work. Document files are a different matter. They need to be managed actively or your folders will become cluttered, making it hard to find files.

Selecting files

Before you can do anything with your files, you must select them.

◆   *To select a single file*, point to it or click once on it (depending upon your Folder Options, see page 107).

◆   *To select a set of adjacent files*, if they are in a list or form a rectangular block, click to the side of the top one and drag an outline over the set.

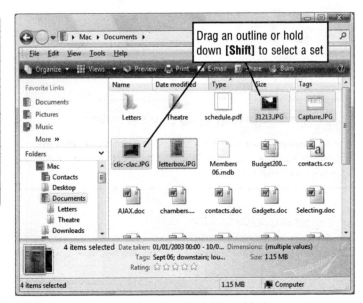

Figure 7.16 Adjacent files can be selected as a block.

Figure 7.17 Scattered files can also be selected together – it's fiddly, but still simpler than repeating operations on individual files.

Or

Select the first, hold down [**Shift**], and select the last.

• *To select scattered files*, select the first, hold down [**Control**] and select the rest in turn.

Will sorting or grouping help?

Remember that files can be arranged in many different ways. If you sorted or grouped the files on a property would it make it easier to select them?

Moving and copying files

Files can be easily moved or copied. The technique is similar for both.

1 Select the file(s).

2 Scroll through the **Folders** display and/or open subfolders, if necessary, until you can see the target folder.

Figure 7.18 If you can see the target folder, you can drag files into it.

3 Drag the file(s) across the screen and over the target folder to highlight it, then drop the file(s) there.

◆ If the original and target folders are both on the same disk, this will move the selected file(s).

◆ If the folders are on different disks, or your target is a floppy disk, this will copy the file(s).

To move a file from one disk to another, or copy within the same disk, hold down the right button while you drag. When you release the button, select **Move** or **Copy** from the context menu.

If you cannot see the target folder in the Folders list, open a second Explorer window and display it there, then drag the files across the screen between them.

Copy To Folder and Move To Folder

If your mouse control is a bit iffy, things can go astray when dragging files and folders. A slower, but more reliable alternative is to use the **Copy To Folder** and **Move To Folder** commands.

1 Select the file(s).

2 To move a file, open the **Edit** menu and select **Move to Folder...**

Or

3 To copy, open the **Edit** menu and select **Copy to Folder...**

4 The **Move/Copy Items** dialog box will open. Work your way down through the folder structure and select the target folder, then click **OK**.

- If you copy a file into the same folder, it will be renamed 'Copy of...' (the original filename).

Renaming files

If you want to edit or retype a file's name, select the file and press F2 on your keyboard, or use **Rename** from the **File** or context menu.

Change the name as required and press [**Enter**] to fix the new name.

> ### Extensions
>
> When renaming files, do not change their extensions! If you do, you will lose the document-application link (page 110).

Sending files elsewhere

The **Send To** command on the **File** or shortcut menus offers a simple way to copy a file to a floppy disk or to your Mail system for sending by e-mail. Just select the destination to begin.

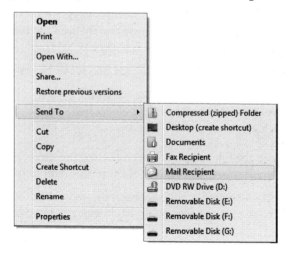

Deleting files

If a file is no longer needed, select it and press [Delete] on your keyboard or use the **File → Delete** command. If you delete a folder, all its files are also deleted.

Windows makes it very difficult to delete files by accident! First, you have to confirm – or cancel – the deletion at the prompt.

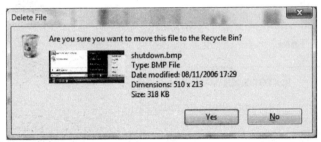

Second, nothing is permanently deleted at this stage. Instead, the file or folder is transferred to the Recycle Bin. Let's have a look at that now.

7.10 The Recycle Bin

The true value of the Recycle Bin is only fully appreciated by those of us who have used systems which lack this refinement, and have spent hours – or sometimes days – replacing files deleted in error! In practice, you will rarely need the Bin, but when you do, you will be glad that it is there!

If you find that you need a deleted file, it can be restored easily.

1 Open the Recycle Bin, from the Desktop icon or in Windows Explorer (at the end of the Folders list).

2 Select the file(s).

3 Open the **File** menu, or right-click for the shortcut menu and select **Restore**, or click the **Restore this item** button.

• If the file's folder has also been deleted, it will be re-created first, so that the file can go back where it came from.

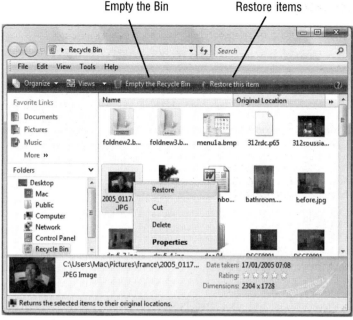

Empty the Bin   Restore items

Figure 7.19 Files deleted in error can be restored from the Bin.

One of the main reasons for deleting files is to free up disk space, but as long as they are in the Recycle Bin, they are still on the disk. So, make a habit of emptying the bin from time to time.

• There is an **Empty the Recycle Bin** button on the toolbar, and an **Empty...** option on the **File** menu (when no files are selected). But only empty the bin when you are absolutely sure that there is nothing in it that you might want to restore.

• Play safe! Always open the Bin, check its contents and restore any accidental deletions, before you use the **Empty Recycle Bin** command.

- The default settings allows the Recycle Bin to use up to 10% of the drive's capacity, which should work well. If you want to change this, right-click on the Bin's icon to open its Properties panel and set the level there.

7.11 Searching for files

Windows Explorer has a neat Search utility, which can track down lost files for you, hunting for them by name, location, tags, contents, date, type and/or size. If you organize your folders properly, and always store files in the right places, you'll never need this utility. However, if you are like me, you will appreciate it.

A simple search can be by all or part of the filename, or the content of text files (in indexed folders). Here's how to find a file if you can remember what it was called, or a keyword in it, but not where you stored it.

1 In the Folders or Favorites lists in Explorer, select the highest level folder that it could be in. The search routine will go through all its subfolders.

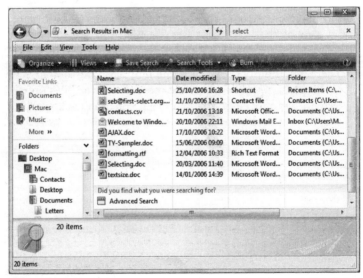

Figure 7.20 The results of simple search – note the Advanced Search link at the bottom of the results.

2 Click into the **Search** box and type all or part of the name or of a significant word in its text. Almost as soon you start to type, the search results will be displayed in the Contents Pane. Type more of the filename, the the results will be filtered further, reducing the number of matching files.

3 Double-click on the file to open it, or make a note of its folder so that you can find it easily again later.

If the simple search doesn't find the file...

1 Click the **Advanced Search** link at the bottom of the results.

2 In the **Show only** bar at the top, select the type of file.

3 In the **Location**, select the highest-level folder, or the disk drive, *Everywhere* if you haven't a clue where it might be.

4 To filter by **Date**, select modified, created or accessed, then select **Is** and set the range, or **Is before/after** and set the date.

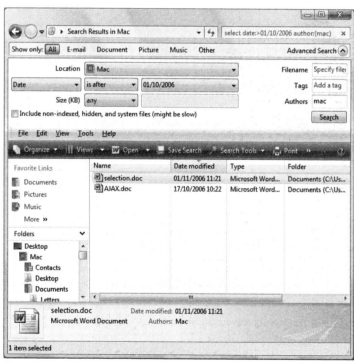

Figure 7.21 Running an advanced search.

5 To filter by **Size**, select equals, less than or greater than and set the limit.

6 Type part or all of the filename, tags or author.

7 Click [Search].

Summary

- Folders on disks create organized storage for your files.

- Windows Explorer is the main utility for managing files and folders, and has a comprehensive set of tools.

- The View options allow you to set up the display to suit yourself.

- You should create folders for each area of your computer work. Folders can be created within other folders.

- Desktop shortcuts can be created by dragging file or folder icons from Explorer onto the Desktop.

- You can give files tags, which can be used when sorting or searching for files.

- Files can be displayed in various views and can be sorted, grouped or filtered by name, size, type, tag, date order or other properties.

- To create a file association, select the application when Windows asks you what it should open a document with.

- To select sets of files, drag an outline with the mouse, or use the mouse in combination with [Shift] or [Ctrl].

- Files can be moved, copied, renamed or deleted.

- When renaming files, do not change the extensions, as these identify the type of document.

- The Send command offers a simple way to copy a file to a floppy disk, or to e-mail it to someone.

- When a file is deleted, it is transferred to the Recycle Bin. If necessary, files can be restored from the Bin.

- The Search routine allows you to track down files through their name (or part of it!), location, date, type or size.

08 control panel

In this chapter you will learn:

- about the Control Panel
- how to remove programs
- how to configure the mouse and the keyboard
- about the clock, language and regional settings
- about the Ease of Access Center
- how to add user accounts

8.1 Using the Panel

Windows' plug and play facility for new hardware, and the installation routines for new software, help to ensure that your system is properly configured. However, there are some things which Windows cannot do for you as they depend upon your preferences. The Control Panel is where you find the tools to customize your setup to suit yourself. In this chapter we will be looking at eight of the key components. Even if you are happy with the way that your system is running – or if you are hesitant about making changes that you might regret – do have a look at these. All the dialog boxes have a **Cancel** button!

◆ To open the Control Panel, click the **Start** button then click its link on the right-hand side.

The panel has two alternative displays:

◆ The default view (Figure 8.1) is probably the best view for new users. It groups the components by function and guides you through the tasks.

◆ **Classic View** (Figure 8.2) will be familiar to users of earlier versions of Windows. It display all the components, and for the most part – though not always – it is obvious which you should use to customize which part of your PC.

We'll work through the default Vista view.

See also

Some of the Control Panel options are dealt with in other contexts, elsewhere in the book.

For the Display aspects of Appearance and Personalization, see Chapter 6.

For the Taskbar and Start menu, see Chapter 9.

Folder Options were covered in Section 7.7.

For the Internet, see Chapter 12.

For System and Maintenance, see Chapter 10.

For Printers, see Chapter 11.

Figure 8.1 The Control Panel in the default view

Figure 8.2 The Control Panel in Classic View. Even if you are new to Windows with Vista, you may find it worthwhile switching to this as it does give you a direct route to the components – and it is usually pretty obvious what each component does.

8.2 Programs

Any software that is written to the Windows specifications will be registered with the system when it is installed, so that it can be uninstalled, or the installation adjusted later through this facility.

Uninstall or change a program

Use this to clear unwanted software off your system, or to add or remove components from suites, such as Microsoft Office. If you simply delete a program's folder in Explorer, it may remove all or most of the software's files – though there may be others scattered elsewhere in your disks – but it will not remove the entry in the Start menu, or the File Types associations. A proper uninstall will (normally) do a full clean-out from your system.

1   In the **Programs** list, click **Uninstall a program**.

2   At the **Uninstall or change programs** dialog box, select the program.

3   With most programs you will now see an **Uninstall/Change** button in the toolbar – click it. (Some Microsoft applications also have a **Repair** option.)

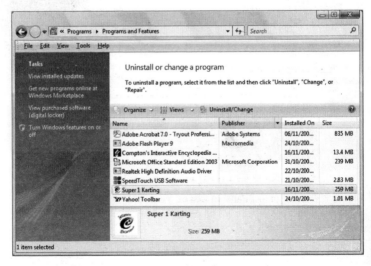

Figure 8.3 Starting to uninstall a program.

4 The uninstall routines vary between programs, but you will normally be asked to confirm before the program is uninstalled.

Windows features

Windows Vista is a huge package with a vast set of utilities and accessories – most people will use only a limited number of these and no one will use all of them. You may decide, after having used Windows for a while, that some components are a waste of space – and then again, you may need to put them back later!

1 In the **Uninstall or change programs** dialog box, click the **Turn Windows features on and off** link in the Tasks list on the left.

The components are listed, with a checkbox beside the name to indicate its status, and a disk space given on the right. The checkboxes can be in one of three states:

☑ all components selected under this heading

▣ some components selected

☐ no components selected.

2 A ⊞ icon beside a heading shows that it has subcomponents – click on the icon to display them.

3 Tick the checkbox to add a component, or clear it to remove an existing one.

Figure 8.4 Adjusting the Windows Setup.

4   Click **OK** when you have finished and wait while Windows adds or removes components. You may have to restart the PC for some changes to take effect.

8.3   Mouse

We configured the mouse pointers back in Chapter 6. That was just decorative – other aspects of the mouse are more important.

• In the **Hardware and Sound** section, click **Mouse**.

Buttons

The first tab of the **Mouse Properties** panel is for the **Buttons**.

If you are left-handed, you may be tempted by the **Switch primary and secondary buttons** option (so you would use the one on the right for a simple click, and left-click to open context menus). Resist the temptation. It may make life easier when you first start to use your new PC, but you will be in a mess if you ever have to

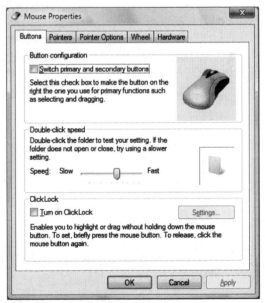

Figure 8.5 When the double-click speed is right for you, you should be able to open and close the test icon easily.

use anybody else's. Get used to the standard setting – it's not hard, I use my mouse with either hand.

The only crucial setting here is the **Double-click** speed. Test the current setting by double-clicking on the folder, and use the slider to adjust the response if necessary.

If you have trouble holding down a button while dragging, you might like to try turning on the **ClickLock** facility. Tick the checkbox then click the Settings button and set the time to wait before turning a 'click' into a 'lock'.

Pointer Options

The **Motion** area controls how far and how fast the pointer moves in relation to the mouse movement. To test this, move the mouse and watch the pointer. If you don't feel comfortably in control of it, drag the slider towards **Slow**. If it's taking too long to get around, set it faster. Click **OK** when it feels right.

Under **Visibility**, you might want to turn on **Pointer trails** if you are working on a laptop PC. Pointers do not show up well on

Slower pointers are
easier to control!

Trails make pointers
more visible – tick
the box and move
the mouse to see
what a trail looks like

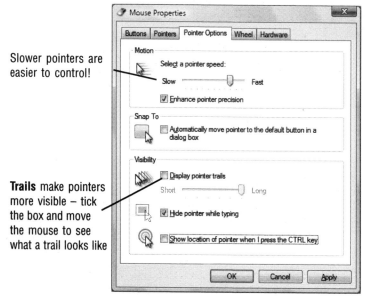

Figure 8.6 The Pointer Options tab controls pointer speed and visiblity.

some LCD screens, particularly when they are in motion. Turning on the trail makes them much easier to see. Likewise, turning on **Show location of pointer** can be handy if you have trouble finding it. With it on, when you press [**Control**] a circle will appear around the pointer and shrink onto it.

On the Wheel tab you can set the scrolling speed of the wheel.

8.4 Keyboard

The Keyboard dialog box is found in **Hardware and Sounds**.

* Click on the main **Keyboard** link, and make sure that the **Speed** tab is at the front.

How long your fingers linger on the keys affects the way that keystrokes are repeated. You normally want keystrokes to be picked up separately, but will sometimes want them to repeat – perhaps to create a line of ******.

* The **Repeat delay** is how long to wait before starting to repeat – if you are heavy-fingered, set this to *Long*.

The cursor blink rate affects the line cursor that is used working with text

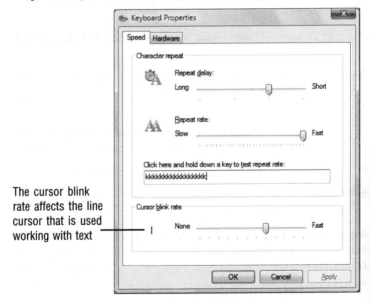

Figure 8.7 Use the Keyboard panel to set the speed to suit you.

- The **Repeat rate** is how fast the characters are produced. This should match your reaction times.

Test the settings by typing in the test area, before you click **OK**.

If you want to increase the thickness of the cursor, go to the **Ease of Access Center** and look for this setting in the **Make the computer easier to see** section.

8.5   Clock, Language and Region

Change the date and time

Even if you do not display the Clock in the Notification Area of the Taskbar (see page 143), you should still make sure that the clock/calendar is correctly set if you want the date and time details to be right on your saved documents. PCs are good time-keepers – Windows even adjusts for Summer Time automatically – as long as they are set correctly at the start.

1   Go to the **Clock, Language and Region** area and select **Date and time**.

2   At the **Date and Time** dialog box, click the **Change date and time** button.

3   To change the date, click on the month/year heading then pick the month from the full year display. Set the day by clicking on it.

4   To change the time, select the hour or minute figure and type the correct value, or use the little arrows to adjust the values.

5   Click **OK** to return to the **Date and Time** dialog box.

6   If you need to change the time zone click the **Change time zone** button and select the zone from the drop-down list.

If you use the PC to connect to the Internet, you can keep your clock accurate by turning on the synchronization option on the **Internet Time** tab. The PC will then synchronize regularly with an Internet time server.

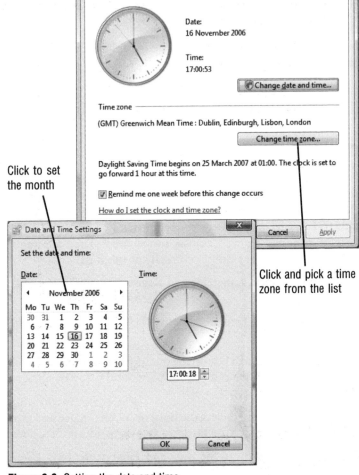

Click to set
the month

Click and pick a time
zone from the list

Figure 8.8 Setting the date and time.

Date, time and number formats

In the Clock, Language and Region area, under **Regional and Language Options** you will find **Change the date, time or number formats**. On the **Regional Options** tab you will see samples of the formats currently used for numbers, currency, time and dates. If you are happy to use the formats that are standard for your region, then all you need to do is select the country from the **Current format** drop-down list.

If you want to vary any of the settings, click **Customize this format** and specify the punctuation and symbols.

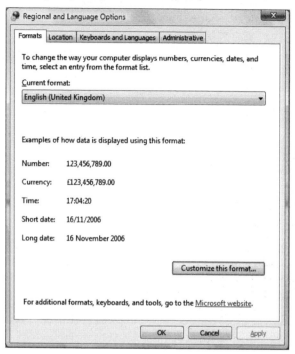

Figure 8.9 Setting the regional options.

8.6 Ease of Access Center

The options here are designed to make life easier for people with disabilities, with the main emphasis on visual disabilities, but there are also other tools that can make life easier for anyone who is less than comfortable with the keyboard or mouse.

Magnifier

This puts a strip across the top of the screen where it displays the active area at anything from twice to 16 times the normal size –

and the active area can be any or all of the mouse position, the current typing location, or wherever any other keys have placed the focus. The depth of the strip can be adjusted, but not its width or position. The settings can be controlled by the panel which appears when you first turn it on, and which can be called up from the Taskbar at any time.

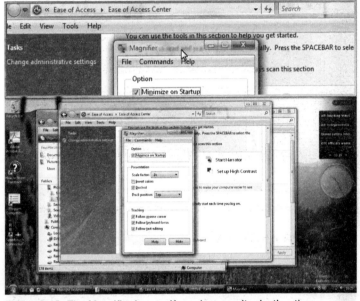

Figure 8.10 The Magnifier in use. If you increase its depth, other windows wil be squashed down to make room.

Narrator

This will read out the text and describe the items beneath the cursor or in dialog boxes and windows when they are opened. There are three alternative voices and you can adjust their speed, pitch and volume.

High Contrast

You can set up the high contrast, large font display so that it can be turned on and off as needed by the key combination [**Shift**] + [**Alt**] + [**Print Screen**].

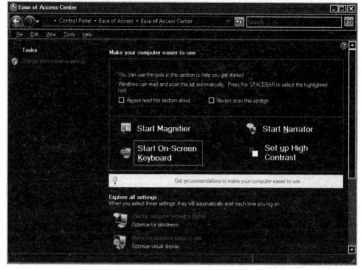

Figure 8.11 The high contrast display can make text easier to read, but can make icon-based work more difficult. Being able to toggle between this and normal is better than setting the screen always to high contrast.

On-screen keyboard

If typing at a keyboard is a problem for any reason, this may be a viable alternative. The on-screen keyboard can be operated by a mouse or other pointing device. As you can only click on one key at a time, the [Shift], [Ctrl] and [Alt] keys are set to remain selected until a second key has been clicked.

By default it sits on top of all other windows, but you can set it to drop beneath the active window. Options on the Keyboard and Settings menus allow you to adjust the layout and how it is used.

Figure 8.12 The on-screen keyboard.

Make the keyboard easier to use

The **Mouse Keys** option lets you use number pad keys to make mouse actions:

[5] does the left click;

[-] and [5] do the right-click;

the remaining number keys move the mouse.

Sticky Keys allow you to get the **Shift, Ctrl** and **Alt** key combinations by pressing them in sequence rather than simultaneously.

Toggle Keys will alert you when the Caps Lock, Num Lock or Scroll Lock keys are pressed. This is handy if, like me, you sometimes hit Caps Lock when aiming for Tab, and then type merrily on in CAPITALS!

Filter Keys control the point at which a keystroke is picked up, or is repeated, and the repeat rate. Most of these settings can also

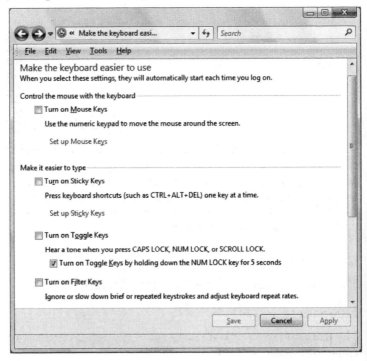

Figure 8.13 Configuring the keyboard for easier access.

be controlled through the Keyboard component (page128). If you still find that the keys are not responding as you would like after you have set the options there, come back and check out Filter Keys.

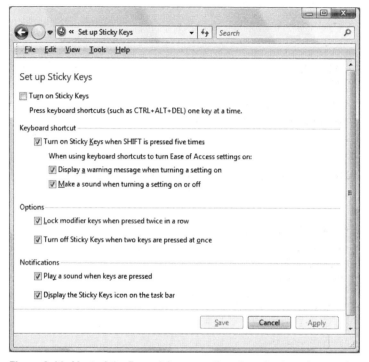

Figure 8.14 Most of the Ease of Access options have Settings that can be configured to your needs – these are the Settings options Sticky Keys. Notice that all Settings panels have a Keyboard shortcut option. If used, the feature can be turned on and off – either to suit different users, or to suit the way you are working at that time.

Mouse settings

The mouse settings can also be adjusted from here.

Alternatives to sounds

The main option on this tab turns on visual clues to replace, or emphasize sound prompts.

8.7 User Accounts

Windows Vista makes it easy for several people to share the use of one PC. Each user can have their own set of folders and their own customized Desktop and Start menu.

You can only create accounts if you have an Adminstrator level account, or if yours is the only account.

1 In the **User Accounts** area in the Control Panel, click **Add or remove a user account.** You will be asked for your permission – click **Continue.**

2 Click **Create a new account.**

Figure 8.15 The User Accounts panel.

3 Enter the user's name and click **Next.**

4 Set the account type. This should be Standard unless the user needs to be able to add software, or add users or make other changes to the system.

5 Click **Create Account.** The new user can later set or change their password or change their picture.

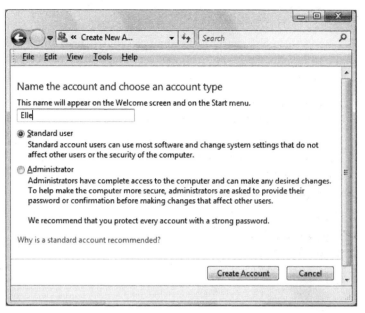

Figure 8.16 Users should normally be set as Standard.

Figure 8.17 The User Accounts panel for a standard user. Passwords should only be created if needed – they can be a pain if forgotten!

Parental Controls

Windows Vista gives parents the ability to control how and when children use the computer. You can set controls on the sorts of websites that they can visit, the times they can use the computer, what games they can play and which programs they can use.

1 In the **User Accounts and Family Safety** area, click **Set up parental controls**.

2 Click on the child's account.

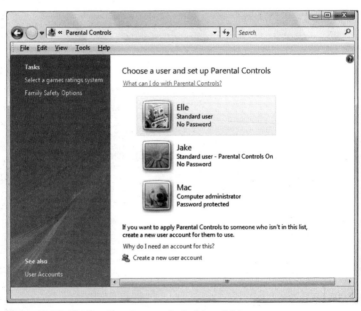

Figure 8.18 Starting to set up controls for a child user.

3 Turn on parental controls, and activity reporting, if wanted.

4 Go to each Windows Settings section in turn. Choose the level of restrictions that you think is appropriate and click **OK**.

5 Back at the main set-up screen, click **OK** to apply the new settings.

The settings can be adjusted at any time to reflect the child's growing maturity.

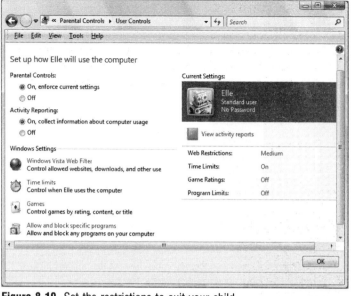

Figure 8.19 Set the restrictions to suit your child.

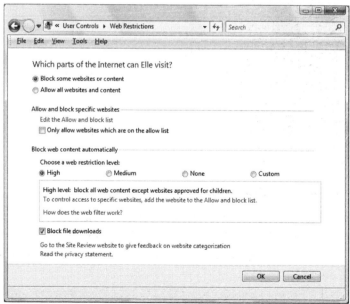

Figure 8.20 Children need protection when on the Web – there are too many sites that they shouldn't see and that they can reach by accident.

Summary

♦ You can configure your system to suit your way of working through the components of the Control Panel.

♦ Use Programs and Features to add or remove the components of application suites and of Windows.

♦ Use the Mouse panel to set the double-click response and the speed at which the mouse moves the pointer.

♦ Test and adjust the response rate of the keyboard through the Keyboard panel.

♦ You can change the date or time, through the Date/Time panel.

♦ The Ease of Access Center options can make the keyboard easier to use and the screen easier to see.

♦ If several people use the PC, you can set up and configure separate, secure user accounts for them.

♦ Parental Controls can be set on accounts if wanted.

09

taskbar and start menu

In this chapter you will learn:

- how to control the Taskbar display
- how to add toolbars to the Taskbar
- how to customize the Start menu

9.1 Taskbar options

By now you should be familiar with using the Taskbar and Start menu in your Windows sessions. Here we will look at ways in which you can customize the Taskbar and reorganize the Start menu. The techniques are simple and worth learning – these are two elements of the Windows system that you use regularly, so you should have them set up to your way of working. The Properties panel for the Taskbar and Start Menu can be opened by right-clicking on the Taskbar or the Start button and selecting **Properties**.

On the **Taskbar** tab you will see six on/off options which affect its appearance and working in various ways.

• **Lock the taskbar** – fixes the current position of the Taskbar and of its toolbars. Unlock it if you want to adjust the layout.

Figure 9.1 Setting the Taskbar options.

- **Auto hide** – if set, the Taskbar slides off-screen when not in use. Pointing off the screen makes it pop-up again. With a small screen, turn this on to maximize the working area.

- **Keep the taskbar on top of other windows** – will ensure that it is visible no matter how you move windows on screen.

- **Group similar taskbar buttons** – if you are running several copies of a program, e.g. Explorer open at various folders, and the Taskbar is crowded, the copies are piled onto one button. Click to open the list to select the copy you want.

- **Show Quick Launch** – displays the Quick Launch toolbar (see page 6) next to the Start button.

The Notification Area holds icons for system programs and for utilities, such as anti-virus software, that work in the background when the PC is running. On the **Notification Area** tab, you can control which icons to display.

Figure 9.2 Setting the Notification Area options.

- **Hide inactive icons** will normally hide all icons that are not currently active, but you can also set icons to be constantly shown or hidden. Click the Customize button to do this.

- The **Clock, Volume** control, **Network** and **Power** (on a laptop) icons are all optional. If you are running a clock gadget, there's not much point in also showing the clock here.

On the Toolbars tab you can select which toolbars are normally displayed on the Taskbar. These can also be controlled from the right-click menu on the Taskbar – which we will now explore.

9.2 Toolbars

In its initial settings, the Taskbar will have two toolbars on it – **Quick Launch** and **Language Bar**. More can be added if you want to be able to start applications from the Taskbar. There are five ready-made toolbars.

- **Address** – enter an Internet address here, and Internet Explorer will start and try to connect to it.

- **Windows Media Player** – a quick start to your entertainment.

- **Links** – carries a set of buttons with Internet addresses, clicking one starts Internet Explorer to make the connection.

- **Tablet PC Input Panel** – for users with a Tablet PC.

- **Desktop** – contains copies of the icons present on the Desktop.

- **Quick Launch** – for starting the main Internet applications.

Right-click on a blank area of the Taskbar to open the short menu

Figure 9.3 Adding toolbars to the Taskbar.

• **Language Bar** – for switching the keyboard settings between different languages.

Toolbar options

The short menu that can be opened from a toolbar contains the usual Taskbar items, plus a small set of options that control the appearance of the toolbar.

View – **Large** or **Small Icons** sets the size.

Open Folder – opens the toolbar's folder so that you can add or remove shortcuts.

Show Text – adds labels to the program icons.

Show Title – shows the toolbar's title.

Close Toolbar – takes it off the Taskbar.

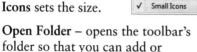

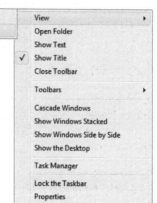

Creating new toolbars

If you like working from the Taskbar, you can set up one or more toolbars containing shortcuts to your favourite applications, folders – or Internet links (see Chapter 12):

1 Create a folder, within *Documents*, and name it 'Tools' or something similar.

2 Set up shortcuts to the chosen applications or folders – hold the right button down as you drag the icons into this folder, and select the **Create Shortcut Here** option.

3 If you are going to show text labels on the toolbar, edit the names so that they are as brief as possible or you will have trouble displaying them all.

4 When you have assembled your shortcuts, right-click on the **Taskbar**, point to **Toolbars** and select **New Toolbar...**

Figure 9.4 Creating a shortcut for the new toolbar. If you want to copy existing shortcuts from the Start menu, hold down the right button and drag them from the menu into the folder, then select **Copy Here**.

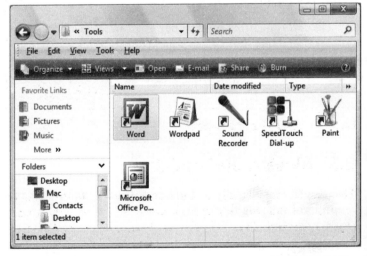

Figure 9.5 The new toolbar folder, almost ready to be added to the Taskbar.

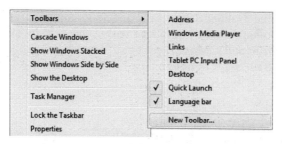

5 Work through the folder display to find the one containing your shortcuts.

6 Click **OK**.

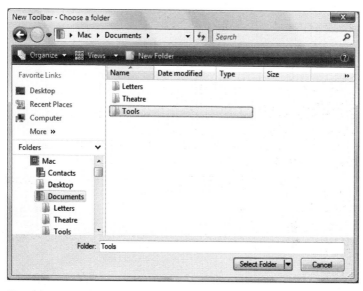

Figure 9.6 Adding the new toolbar.

9.3 Moving and resizing

The Taskbar is normally a thin bar across the bottom of the screen, and this works very well when it is used only for the Quick Launch toolbar and a few application buttons. Add more toolbars and it is going to get crowded and difficult to use. There are two possible solutions:

- Make the Taskbar deeper by dragging its top edge upwards. The toolbars can be rearranged within this area by dragging on their handles. Move them up or down between the lines, or drag sideways to adjust their relative sizes.

Drag the edge to change the depth

Drag on a dotted handle to move a toolbar
or to make it wider/narrower

- Move the Taskbar to one or other side of the screen. By default it will be wide enough to show the Text labels on the icons. You will probably need to adjust the layout by dragging on the handles between the sections, and may want to make the bar slimmer – drag its edge inwards.

Figure 9.7 Moving and resizing the Taskbar.

Do you need labels?

If the icons are clear enough, the toolbar titles and shortcut labels are not really necessary. Turning them off will save a lot of space, allowing you to pack more into a slim Taskbar.

9.4 The Start menu

Right-click on the **Start** button and select **Properties** from the short menu, to go to the **Start Menu** tab of the **Taskbar and Start Menu Properties** panel. Here you can customize the appearance of the menu, and control which items appear on your menu system, and where.

Notice the Privacy options. The list of recently opened files and programs makes it simpler to get back to the last jobs you were doing, but it also makes it easier for other people to see what you have been doing. In an office environment, there could be good reasons why you might want to turn off one or both of the **Store and display** options.

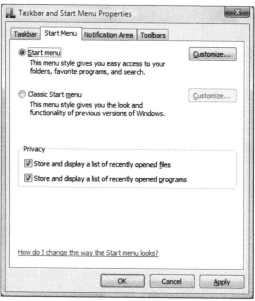

Figure 9.8 The Start Menu Properties panel

The most dramatic change you can make to the menu is to switch to the 'Classic' style – combine this with a Windows Classic screen display and you will have a PC which looks very similar to one running Windows 98. The Classic menu can be customized in just the same way as it can be in earlier versions of Windows, with special routines for adding and removing menu items.

Figure 9.9 The Classic Start menu takes up less screen space (until you open the Programs menu up), but doesn't offer the same quick access to your most-used programs and folders.

Customizing the Start menu

There are some simple, and some slightly more complicated, things you can do to customize the Start menu. We'll begin with the easy stuff!

1 Click **Customize...**

2 You can control which of the standard shortcuts are on the menu, and – in some cases – whether they are displayed as links or menus. Work through the list, setting items to be displayed or not.

3 In the **Start menu size** area you can set how many shortcuts to have in the quick access set on the left.

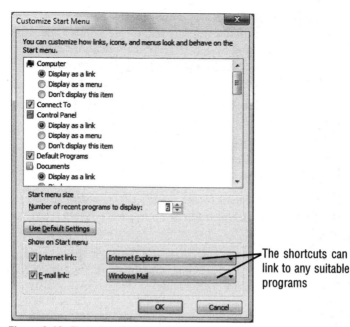

The shortcuts can link to any suitable programs

Figure 9.10 First steps in customizing the Start menu.

4 You can select the programs to run from the **Internet** and the **E-mail** shortcuts, or turn them off if not wanted.

5 Click **OK**.

Tidying the Start menu shortcuts

If you want to remove a single item from the 'most used' program shortcuts, open the Start menu, right-click on the shortcut and select the Remove from This List option.

Reorganizing the menus

The Start menu system is stored as a set of folders and subfolders – or rather, as several sets, as each user has his or her own Start menu. There is also an All Users set that is combined with individual users' sets to produce their menu displays. Within the Start menu are folders for each submenu, and the shortcuts are held as files in these.

If you have installed so many applications that your **All Programs** menu has become overcrowded, create group folders and move the shortcuts and folders of related applications into these. A short main menu that leads to two levels of submenus is easier to work with than one huge menu!

1   Open the Start menu, right-click on **All Programs**.

2   Select **Explore** or **Explore All Users** (if you want to change the common core of the menu).

> | Open |
> | Explore |
> | Search... |
> | Properties |
> | Open All Users |
> | Explore All Users |

▶ **All Programs**

3   When the Start menu folder opens, click **Folders** to display the folder list – it will make it much easier to see what you are doing.

4   Reorganize the menu system, using the normal file management techniques for moving, deleting and renaming files (shortcuts) and folders (submenus).

Figure 9.11 Exploring the folders of the Start menu system. In the example, Windows Explorer is being moved to the main Programs menu – this is a useful program and should be easy to get to.

Summary

- The Taskbar can be displayed on top of all other windows, behind them, or tucked off screen when not in use.

- You can control which icons are displayed in the Notification Area.

- Ready-made toolbars can be added to the Taskbar.

- You can create your own folders of shortcuts and turn them into Taskbar toolbars.

- You can adjust the depth and position of the Taskbar, and move the toolbars within it.

- You can customize the appearance and the selection of shortcuts on the Start menu.

- The menu structure can be reorganized using the normal file management techniques.

10 maintenance

In this chapter you will learn:

- about the need for maintenance
- how Disk Cleanup, Disk Check and Defragmenter can keep your hard disk in good condition
- how to backup and restore files
- about System Restore

10.1 The need for maintenance

Today's hard disks should give you years of trouble-free service. They will, however, give better service if they are maintained properly. Windows Vista has tools that do all the donkey work, once you have started them off – most are designed to be run automatically. Hard disks are now far more reliable than they were only a few years ago – it's unusual for them to become corrupted and lose data, rare for them to crash altogether. But these things do happen, and files can become corrupted through software errors or lost through human error. For these reasons, it is important to protect your valuable data by backing it up – and doing so regularly.

A disk – hard or floppy – is divided into *clusters*, each of which can contain all or part of a file. When a file is first written to a new disk, it will be stored in a continuous sequence of clusters, and the disk will gradually fill up from the start. If a file is edited and resaved – bigger than before – it will overwrite the original clusters then write the remainder in the next available ones, which may well not be physically next to them on the disk. When a file is deleted, it will create a space in the middle of used area, and later that may be filled by a part of another file. Over time disks get messier, with files increasingly stored in scattered clusters. They are still safely stored, but a file that is held in one continuous chunk can be opened much more quickly, simply because the system does not have to chase around all over the disk to read it.

Disk Properties and disk tools

The key maintenance tools can be run from the Properties panel of any disk. Get to know these, and keep your PC healthy.

Disks and drives

These words are often used interchangeably, but strictly speaking, a disk is that flat, round thing on which data is stored, while a drive is a logical area of storage identified by a letter (A:, C:, etc.). The floppy drive or CD/DVD drive can have different disks put into it. A hard disk can be partitioned to create two or more drives.

- Right-click on a drive in Explorer and select **Properties** from the menu, the **Properties** panel will open.

  The **General** tab shows how much used and free space you have on the drive – you can run a clean up from here.

  The **Tools** tab has buttons to start the Error-checker, Disk Defragmenter and Backup.

  The **Previous Versions** tab offers a way to restore files and folders.

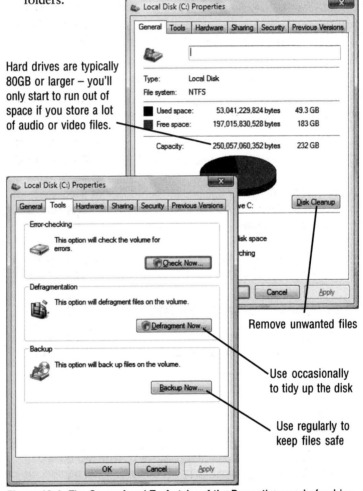

Hard drives are typically 80GB or larger – you'll only start to run out of space if you store a lot of audio or video files.

Remove unwanted files

Use occasionally to tidy up the disk

Use regularly to keep files safe

Figure 10.1 The **General** and **Tools** tabs of the Properties panel of a drive.

10.2 Disk Cleanup

This is the simplest of the system tools, and one that should be run fairly regularly to free up space. It removes temporary and other unwanted files from the hard disk.

When you start Disk Cleanup, if you have an administrator account, you will be asked if you just want to clear your own files, or all potentially unnecessary files. The main types are:

* **Downloaded Program Files** are Java or ActiveX applets (small programs) that you met on Web pages, and which had to be stored on your disk so that they could be run.

* **Temporary Internet Files** – leave these if you want to be able to revisit pages without having to go online again.

* **Recycle Bin** – this just saves you having to empty the Bin as a separate operation.

* **Temporary files** are those created by applications, such as automatic backups and print files. They are normally cleaned

Figure 10.2 Disk Cleanup.

up when the application is closed, but may be left behind especially if it ends with a crash. Disk Cleanup will not touch new files, which the application may still be using.

After you have made your selection and clicked **OK**, you will be prompted to confirm the deletion – this is irreversible – before the cleanup starts.

10.3 Disk Check

In earlier versions of Windows, the Disk Check was not simple to run, but offered good control of what to do about any errors that it found. The new error checker is far simpler – in fact, it takes total control. All you can do is select the types of checks.

- With **Automatically fix file system errors** on, the check will try to solve any problems that it meets – and as it will certainly do this better than you or me, I'd leave it to it!

- The **Scan for and attempt recovery of bad sectors** will fix file system errors and test the surface of the disk, to make sure that files can be stored safely, and rebuild it if necessary.

The check will be performed the next time the PC is turned on.

1 Switch to the **Tools** tab of the disk's **Properties** panel and click **Check Now...**

2 Set the options and click **Start**.

3 Click **Schedule disk check** to run one at the next start up.

Figure 10.3 Setting up Disk Check.

10.4 Disk Defragmenter

We noted earlier that the storage space on a disk is divided into clusters, and that a file may occupy any number of clusters, each linked to the next. On a new, clean disk, each file will normally be written in a set of clusters that are physically continuous on the disk. Over time, as the disk fills up, and as files are written, rewritten (larger or smaller) and deleted, it gradually becomes more difficult to store files in adjacent clusters – the disk is becoming *fragmented*. The files are still safe, but they cannot be read as quickly if the reading heads have to hop all over the disk.

Disk Defragmenter reorganizes the physical storage of files on the disk, pulling together the data from scattered clusters. Though it improves performance, the gains are in the order of a few seconds for starting a program or loading a data file, and it is a very slow job – allow an hour or more on a 80Gb disk. It is only worth doing regularly if your disk is getting full – so that new files are being stored in a limited area – or if you have a high turnover of files from working on large databases or multimedia files, or from installing and removing demos, shareware and other programs.

There is nothing to see when the defragmenter is working, and it works best if the disk is not being used by anything else at the same time. The most efficient solution is to run it on a schedule, at a time when you will not be using the PC.

1 Open the **Tools** tab of the disk's **Properties** panel and click **Defragment Now...**

2 If you are about to end your session anyway, and won't want to use the PC for a while, click [**Defragment now**].

Otherwise

3 Click **Modify schedule...**

4 Use the drop-down lists to set *How often*, *What day* and *What time* the defragmener is to run, then click **OK**.

5 Click **OK** to close the Defragmenter window.

6 Make a note of the time and day when you should leave your PC on so that the Defragmenter can run.

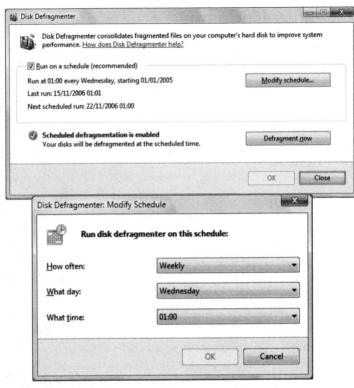

Figure 10.4 Setting the schedule for defragmenting.

10.5 Backup

If an application's program files become corrupted or accidentally deleted, it is a nuisance but not a major problem as you can simply reinstall the application from the original disks. Data files are a different matter. How much is your data worth to you? How long would it take you to rewrite that report, redraw that picture or re-enter the last six months' accounts if they were lost? Individual files can be copied onto floppies for safekeeping, but if you have more than one or two it is simpler to use Backup. A backup job is easily set up, doesn't take long to run and will more than pay for itself in time and trouble the first time that you need it!

Backup media

Backups can be done on optical disks – CDs or DVDs – and these should be fine for home use or in a small business where there's not a huge quantity of data. You can get 700MB on a CD, or if you need more capacity than that, DVDs can hold from 4.7GB to 17GB, depending upon their type.

Rewritable disks are a little more expensive than write-once disks, but usually pay their way over time. With a single use CD or DVD, once you have stored data on the disk – no matter how little – the disk cannot be reused. With a rewritable disk, you can write to it again and again, until it is quite full. CDs and DVDs are not rewritable in the same way as magnetic disks. The files on those can be erased or overwritten by new data. Once data has been written onto an optical disk, that part of the surface cannot be written on again. What makes them 'rewritable' is that the index can be rewritten and additional material stored in later sessions.

Whatever you save on must be removable. You must be able to store the backup away from the machine – in a fireproof safe or a different building if you want real security.

The Backup routine is easy to use. To set it up, you specify the storage medium, types of files to be stored and the schedule. The first time that you run it, it will perform a complete backup of all the selected file types; in later backups, it will store only those that are new or have been changed.

1 On the **Tools** tab of the disk's **Properties** panel, click **Backup Now...** to run **Backup Status and Configuration**.

2 Click **Change backup settings**.

3 Put the backup CD/DVD into the drive.

4 Select where the backup is to be stored. Notice that you can save on another PC if you are on a network. This may be convenient but is only really safe if the backup PC is in a different building.

5 Tick the types of files you want to store. You cannot select specific files or folders to include or ignore – all files of the selected types will be backed up.

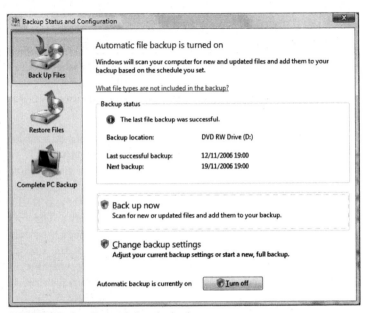

Figure 10.5 Starting to define the backup.

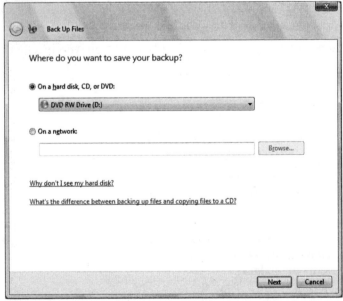

Figure 10.6 You can backup on another hard disk, or on the network, but using removable media is safer.

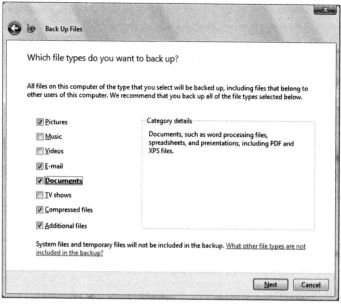

Figure 10.7 If you are not sure what a file type covers, point to it and read the description.

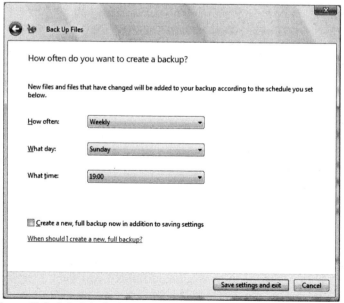

Figure 10.8 Schedule the backup for a quiet time.

6 Set the schedule, specifying how often, what day and what time. Backing up does not generally take that long, and is not that intrusive, but it will be done faster and more efficiently if you are not using the PC at the time.

7 Click **Save settings and exit**.

Restoring files

With any luck this will never be necessary!

1 Run **Backup Status and Configuration**. Click the **Restore Files** button then select **Restore Files** in the main panel.

2 Insert the CD or DVD with the backup into its drive.

3 Click the **Add files...** or **Add folders...** button and select the files and folders you want to restore.

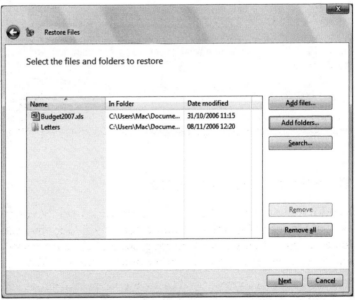

Figure 10.9 Restoring a file from a backup – not difficult, and far, far easier than trying to recreate it from scratch!

4 Restore the file to its original location if you want to replace the existing file with the backup.

Or

5   Select a new location if you want to retain the current versions as well – there may be valuable data in the new file.

6   Click **Start restore** – that's it.

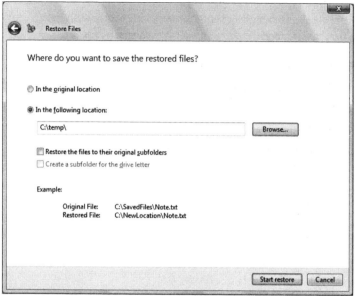

Figure 10.10 Restoring a file to a new location, so that the current copy is not overwritten.

10.6 Previous versions

Even if you can't be bothered to backup your files, Windows can. It automatically keeps 'shadow copies' of your files and folders as part of the system protection (see 10.7, *System Restore*), and you can use these to revert to previous versions of files.

1   Run **Windows Explorer** and locate the file or folder that you want to recover. Right-click and select **Properties** from the context menu.

2   At the Properties panel, switch to the **Previous Versions** tab.

3   Find and select the copy from the last time when the file or folder was in the state you want it to be.

4 You have three choices. Click:

> **Open** to open a file for reading and resaving, or open a folder so that files can be selected for recovery.
>
> **Copy...** to copy the file or folder to a new location.
>
> **Restore...** to replace the original file or folder with the shadow copy.

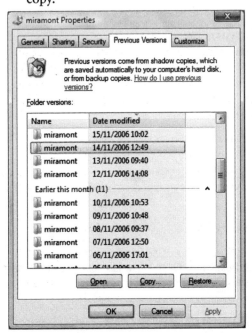

Figure 10.11 Restoring a folder from a previous version. The copies were all created by the daily system restore routine.

10.7 System Restore

With any luck you'll never need this, but it's good to know that it is there. Windows Vista automatically stores a backup copy of your important system files, known as system restore points, at regular intervals. If these files become corrupted for any reason, e.g. 'user error', new software installation problems or hardware failure, then System Restore will get your system running again.

To restore your system:

1 Save any files that you are working on and close any open applications – the PC will have to restart to restore.

2 Open the **Control Panel,** select **System and Maintenance** then the **Backup and Restore Center.**

3 In the lower part of the display you will find three options:

Restore files will recover files from backups (see page 164).

Restore computer is only to be used in cases of desperation, perhaps after a major virus attack. It will restore your PC to the state it was when you bought it, or when Vista was first installed. Any applications that you have installed since then, and every document that you have created, will be erased from the hard drive.

Use System Restore to fix problems allows you to restore your Windows setup and applications to an earlier stage, but without affecting your data files. It would typically be used when installing new hardware or software has made the system unstable.

Click the link to **Use System Restore...**

4 At the next panel, if you don't want to use the recommended restore point – the latest – then select **Choose a different restore point** and pick the most recent time when you know that the system was running properly.

5 Click **Next,** then **Finish** at the last panel to start the restore. The PC will shut down, then restart using system files as they were at the selected restore point.

Creating a restore point

Windows normally creates a restore point every day, but you can create additional ones if needed. A Vista system is robust, and modern software and hardware is normally reliable and well tested, but things do go wrong. Before you do anything which might upset the system, such as installing new kit or making any other major changes, create a restore point. It takes only a few minutes and could save you endless hours of pain!

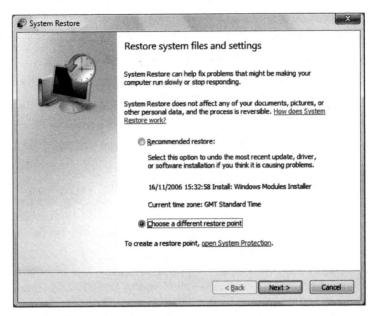

Figure 10.12 Starting a System Restore.

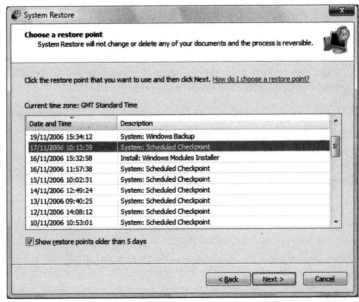

Figure 10.13 Select the last time when you are confident things were OK.

1 Open the **Control Panel,** select **System and Maintenance** then **System.** In the Tasks list, click **System protection.**

2 Click the **Create...** button near the bottom of the panel.

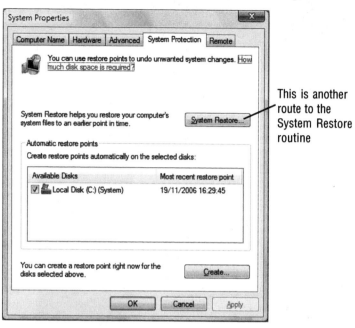

This is another route to the System Restore routine

3 Type in a description to help you identify it – the point will have the date and time added, so this is not too crucial.

4 Click **Create** to start the process.

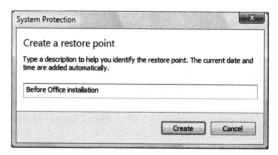

10.8 The System Tools

The utilities that we have been looking at in this chapter can also be reached from the **Start** button. Most are in the **Programs** → **Accessories** → **System Tools** folder, though you will find **Backup and Restore** in the Maintenance set. Open the System Tools and Maintenence folders to see what's there – you may have slightly different sets from those shown here.

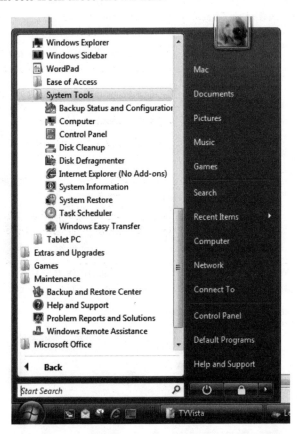

Figure 10.14 The system tools can all be reached through the Start menu.

Summary

* Hard disks need regular maintenance to keep them in good condition. Windows XP provides tools for this.

* The maintenance utilities can be started from the Tools tab of a disk's Properties panel.

* Disk Cleanup will remove temporary and unwanted files.

* Use Disk Check regularly to ensure that your files and folders are intact and correctly stored.

* Disk Defragmenter will reorganize the disk so that files are stored in continuous sequences for faster reading.

* Backup will help you to keep organized copies of your files. Use it regularly. You may never need it, but if you do, you'll be glad that your backups are there!

* You can revert to the previous version of a file using a shadow copy stored by the system.

* System Restore can help to recover the system from calamity.

* The full set of maintenance utilities can be found in the System Tools and Maintenance folders in the Start menu.

printers

In this chapter you will learn:

- how to add a printer
- about printer properties
- how to print from applications
- how to control the print queue
- how to print from files

11.1 Adding a new printer

Many printers are 'plug and play' – just connect them, and Windows will configure the system so that they can be used. Sometimes you need to install the drivers – the programs that convert the PC's formatting codes into ones for the printer – and there is normally software to control and configure the printer. Here we look at how to manage printers and how to install those that aren't plug and play.

If your printer dates from before Vista's release at the start of 2007, the drivers available in Windows Vista will probably be newer than those supplied with the printer. If it is more recent, dig out its installation disk.

1 Open the **Control Panel,** and select **Printers** in the **Hardware and Sound** area.

2 Click **Add a printer** to start the installation.

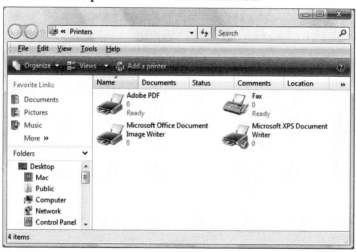

Figure 11.1 Some 'printers' do not actually print. This set also includes a fax and a PDF creator.

3 At the first screen, select *Local printer*, if it is attached to your PC, or *Network printer* if you access it through a network.

4 For a local printer, you then choose the port – normally LPT1.

5 For a network printer, browse to find the one you want.

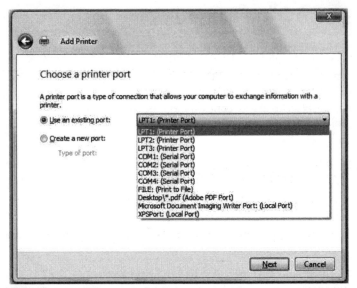

Figure 11.2 Selecting a port. COM ports are used for modems and the like.

6 To use one of the Windows Vista drivers, select the **Manufacturer** from the list, then the **Printer** model. If an installation disk came with the printer, click **Have Disk.**

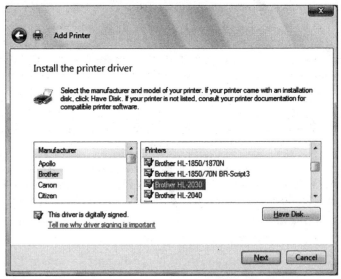

Figure 11.3 Vista has drivers for virtually all printers currently in use.

7 You may want to edit the full manufacturer/model name into something shorter to label the icon in the Printers folder.

8 If you have more than one printer, one is set as the *default* – the one to use unless you specify otherwise when you start printing.

9 At the final stage, accept the offer of a test print – it's as well to check! Click **Finish** to close the installation window.

11.2 Printer Properties

Before you use the printer, check its properties. If nothing else, you may need to change the paper size, as it is often set to the US Letter. The standard UK paper size is A4 (210 × 297mm).

Right-click on the new icon in the Printers folder and select **Properties**. Different printers have different Properties panels, but you should find:

- A **General** tab, where you can type a comment. This is mainly useful on a network, to tell others of any special requirements that you or the printer have.

- An **Advanced** tab, where you can select a new driver if needed. The **Spool** settings determine whether the file is sent directly from the application to the printer, or through a temporary memory buffer. Spooling frees up applications, as they can generally send data out faster than the printer can handle it.

- A **Printing Defaults** or **Preferences** button, which leads to a dialog box where you can set the paper size. The other options here are best left at their defaults, though you may want to change them before printing specific documents.

- A **Device Settings** panel. Check the **Memory** (normally only with laser printers). If you have added extra memory – a good idea if you print pages with lots of graphics – tell Windows.

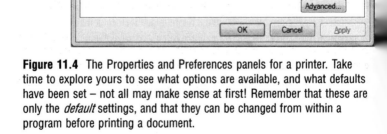

Figure 11.4 The Properties and Preferences panels for a printer. Take time to explore yours to see what options are available, and what defaults have been set – not all may make sense at first! Remember that these are only the *default* settings, and that they can be changed from within a program before printing a document.

11.3 Printing from applications

The Print routines in applications are all much the same. There will usually be a 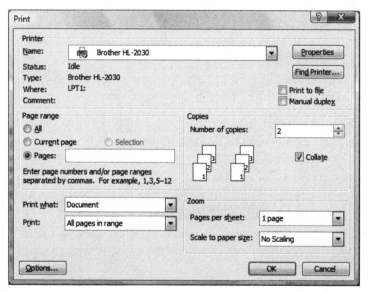 toolbar button, and clicking on this will send the document to the printer using its current settings – whatever they are.

- The first time that you print something, it is best to start by selecting **Print** from the **File** menu. This will open a dialog box where you can define the settings – the key ones are which pages to print and how many copies.

Figure 11.5 The Print dialog box from Word. Other applications have different options, but Page range and Copies are common to all. Note the Collate option. When you print multiple copies, turning this on may make printing take longer, but you won't have to sort a pile of paper afterwards.

If you need to change the layout, print quality or other printer settings, clicking the **Properties** button will open the printer's properties panel – this may look slightly different from the panel opened from the Printers folder, but gives you access to the same settings.

11.4 Controlling the print queue

Unless you are very disorganized or have unreliable hardware, most of your printing will run smoothly. But things go wrong even at the most organized and best equipped desk, and problems between printers and PC are not uncommon.

When a document is sent for printing, it goes first to the print queue. If it is the only print job, it is then processed directly. If not, it will sit in the queue and wait its turn. As long as a document is still in the queue, you can do something about it – but if it is just one short, simple document, it will almost certainly be through the queue before you can get to it.

+ If you discover a late error, so that printing is just a waste of paper, a job can be cancelled.

+ If you have sent a series of documents in succession, you can change the order in which they are printed.

When the printer is active, you will see 🖨 in the Notification Area on the right of the Taskbar. Right-click on it.

Select the printer to open its folder, where the queue is stored.

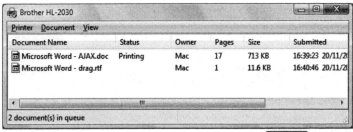

+ *To cancel a print job*, select the document, then use **Cancel** from the **Document** menu.

- *To cancel all the queued jobs*, use **Cancel All Documents** from the **Printer** menu.

- Use **Pause Printing** if you need time to restock the paper or replace the ink or toner.

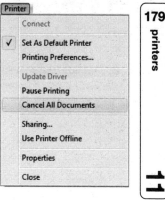

Don't just turn off! Turning off the printer is not a good way to stop a print job. If the document is partially printed or waiting in the queue it will start to print again as soon as the printer is turned back on – and if partially printed, the output when it restarts will be probably be garbled. You must clear the queue to get rid of a print job.

- *To change the order of printing*, select a document and drag it up or down the queue as required – this only works with those documents that are not already being spooled or printed.

11.5 Printing from file

You can print a document from Windows Explorer, as long as you have an application which can handle it. Windows will open the application, print the document, then close the application for you.

To send the document to the default printer:

- Select the file and click the **Print** button on the toolbar.

Or

- Right-click on the file and select **Print** from the short menu.

Figure 11.6 You can print a document directly from file.

Summary

+ To install a new printer, use the Add Printer routine in the Printers folder. Windows Vista has drivers for almost every known printer model.

+ Check the printer's Properties panel before use, to make sure that the default settings – especially the paper size – are suitable.

+ When printing from an application, you can usually set the page range and number of copies. If required, the printer Properties can be adjusted before printing.

+ Documents are taken to the print queue before output. By opening the queue you can cancel a print job or change the order in which they are printed.

+ A document can be printed directly from Windows Explorer.

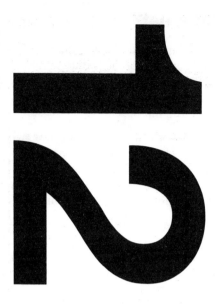

12

internet explorer

In this chapter you will learn:

- about getting online
- hot to use and configure Internet Explorer
- how to browse and search the Web
- how to find and download files

12.1 What is the Internet?

This chapter concentrates on setting up and using Internet Explorer. We will have a brief look at some of the facilities that can be reached through the Internet, but there isn't room in this book to tackle this huge area properly. If you want to know more about the Internet, try *Teach Yourself The Internet*.

First of all, the Internet is *not* the World Wide Web – they are two different, but intertwined things. The **Internet** is the hardware – the computers and their connections – and the software that allows them to communicate with each other. The **Web** is one way in which information and services are shared over the Internet.

Over 50 million computers (and more every day) are permanently connected to the Internet and offer services to its users. Some of these *hosts* store information – text, pictures, sound or video files; some hold programs that visitors can run; some are connections, passing on messages between computers; some are servers at service providers, allowing ordinary users – you and me – to connect to the Internet and to store our Web pages. And when you go online, your computer becomes part of the Internet.

The host computers are owned and managed by governments, businesses, universities and other organizations. The connections between them are a mixture of public and private telephone lines, cables and microwave links. No single organization that owns or controls the Internet – about the nearest thing you have to central control are the agencies which allocate names to Web sites. It may sound a bit chaotic, but it works!

The Internet started as a 1960s US government project to develop a communications system that could survive a nuclear attack. Fortunately, it has never been tested in full(!) and just as fortunately it was allowed to expand. It spread first into military and research establishments within the USA and overseas, linking the networks in each organization into an *internetwork*. Some US universities set up their own internetwork links, and these joined into the Government's net in the mid-1980s to form the core of the Internet. Since then, it has expanded enormously, so that now most of the world's universities and schools, all big businesses and most smaller ones, most governments and many political parties, pressure groups and charities, are online.

The important thing is that the Internet was not set up as a commercial venture. Even today, when many businesses are advertising and selling goods and services on the Internet, a large part of it remains non-commercial. Much of the data that flows across the Net is generated by people having fun – sharing ideas and tracking down information on their enthusiasms, keeping in touch with remote friends, old and new, playing games, or just plain 'surfing' to see what they can find.

12.2 Getting online

Windows Vista PCs are usually Internet-ready. Most new laptops are Wi-Fi enabled, i.e. they have a built-in wireless broadband modem and the necessary software so that they can connect to any available wireless network. Desktop PCs do not usually have a built-in modem, but that's because the manufacturers expect you to sign up for a broadband connection, and the ISP (Internet Service Provider) will supply the modem.

Exactly how you set up a connection depends upon which ISP you use, but it will normally be very straightforward – there will be an installation CD and a booklet. Follow the instructions, and you should be up and running and online within minutes.

If broadband is not available where you live, you will have to use a dial-up account, and you will need a standard modem. This should cost you around £50 and is easily added – just plug it into a spare USB port. Your dial-up provider should supply you with an installation CD, but if they don't, Windows Vista has a wizard that will help you set up your end of the connection – look in the Connect to the Internet area of the Welcome Center.

12.3 Internet Explorer

You can access the Internet from many places in the Windows Vista system, but the main tool for this job is Internet Explorer. It is very similar to Windows Explorer. In fact, if you use the Favorites, Links buttons or Address bar to connect to a website through Windows Explorer, it will turn into Internet Explorer.

- Microsoft would like you to view the Internet as an extension of your Desktop. If you connect through an always-on broadband line, then this is a viable view. If you connect by dialling in to a service provider, the transition from Desktop to Internet will rarely be smooth or swift.

Internet Explorer is designed for fast, easy navigation, both on and offline. When you browse a page, its files are stored in a temporary folder on your hard disk. When you return to the same page, its files are then loaded from the disk, rather than downloaded from the Internet. This can make browsing far quicker, as you often find that you want to go back and have another look at a page, to read it more closely or to pick up new leads.

The Internet Explorer window

- The **Address bar** shows you where you are. You can type an address here to go to a Web page. At the end of the bar:

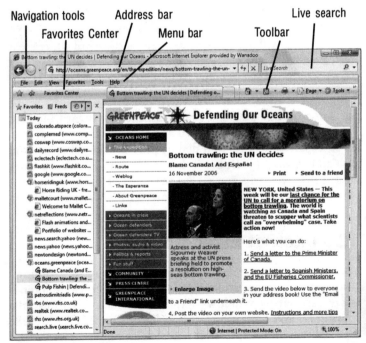

Figure 12.1 The Internet Explorer window.

Refresh will reload the current page – click this if the page stalls when loading in.

Stop – click this when you realize at the start of a long download that you don't really want to see that page.

+ The **Menu bar** is optional – the tools can all be reached through the toolbar.

+ The **Favorites Center** can display Favorites (page 198), History (page 197) or Feeds (see below).

The navigation tools

Use these to move between the pages you have already visited during the session:

+ **Back** takes you to the page you have just left.

+ **Forward** reverses the Back movement.

+ The drop-down page list allows you to select from the last dozen or so pages.

Forward

Back   Last pages visited

The toolbar

These buttons contain almost all of the controls that you need when you are online.

Feeds   Page menu

Home   Print   Tools menu

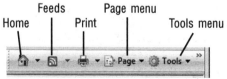

+ **Home** goes to your start page – your jumping off point into the Web. This can be your own home page or any other.

+ **Feeds** are used to alert you to new content in Web pages. Not all sites offer a feeds service – click the button when you are on a page to see if feeds are available from it.

+ **Print** prints the current page (text and graphics).

The Page menu

The commands here are largely concerned with the content of pages. These are worth noting:

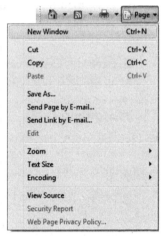

- **Copy** copies text or images for pasting into a document.

- **Save As** stores a copy of the page (see page 200).

- **Send Page/Link by E-mail** connects you to Windows Mail to send the page, or a link to the page, to someone.

- **Zoom** enlarges the text and graphics.

- **Text size** enlarges, or reduces, the text size.

The Tools menu

The key commands to note here are:

- **Pop-up Blocker:** turn this on to block pop-up windows – usually carrying adverts – opening when you visit Web pages.

- **Phishing Filter** should be turned on to restrict those e-mails that try to con you into giving out banking and other personal details.

- **Full screen** removes the toolbars and uses the entire screen to display a page.

- The **Toolbars** submenu controls the display of toolbars and sidebars.

- **Internet Options** allow you to configure Explorer to suit your needs.

12.4 Internet Options

These options can be set or changed at any time on- or off-line (though some only take effect after you restart the PC). A few should be set before you start to use Explorer in earnest, others are best left until you have been using it for a while and have a clearer idea of what settings best suit the way you like to work.

- Use **Tools → Internet Options** to open the panel, and click on the tab names to move between the sets of options.

- If you set options that change the appearance, click **Apply** to see how they look.

- Only click **OK** when you have finished with all the tabs.

General

The **Home page** defines where Internet Explorer goes when it is first started. This could be a personalized start page at your ISP's site (or elsewhere – many sites offer this facility), your own home page, or a blank page if each session is a new voyage. An address can be typed in here, but it is simpler to wait until you are online at the right place, then come to here and click **Use Current**.

In **Temporary Internet files**, click **Settings** to define how Explorer should handle page files.

- In the **Check for newer version of stored pages**, select *Every visit to the page*, if the pages you use a lot change frequently.

- The **Amount of disk space to use** depends upon how much browsing you do, how often you return to pages, how long you like to keep pages in your History and how much space you have. As a general rule, allocate as much space as you can easily spare and see how it goes.

In **Search** you can change to a different search engine from the default Live Search – but give this a try first, it's good!

In **Tabs** you can define how and where new pages open – in tabs or windows. Come back to this after you have spent more time online.

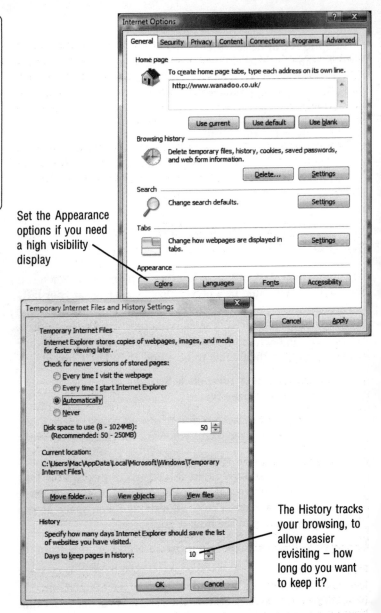

Set the Appearance options if you need a high visibility display

The History tracks your browsing, to allow easier revisiting – how long do you want to keep it?

Figure 12.2 Setting the General options – if you tend to visit pages that have a lot of graphics or information, and you want to be able to study these later, offline, set a high disk space level.

Security and privacy

The Internet is basically a safe place – as long as you take a few sensible precautions. If you spend most of your time at major commercial and other well-established sites, and at ones they recommend, security should not be a major concern. If you browse more widely, you may bump up against the mischievous and the unscrupulous. The main problems are these:

* **Viruses** – You can only get these by running programs or macros in documents. You cannot pick up a virus simply by browsing a page or reading e-mail or news articles. A virus-checker will give you an extra level of protection.

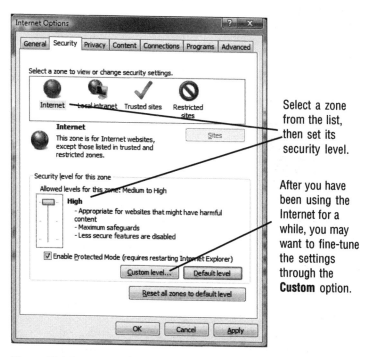

Select a zone from the list, then set its security level.

After you have been using the Internet for a while, you may want to fine-tune the settings through the **Custom** option.

Figure 12.3 The Security tab – when in doubt, play safe! IE sorts sites into four zones: Local intranet, Trusted sites, Restricted sites and Internet (everything else). At first leave the default levels or nudge them a little higher. When you are more aware of what you are likely to meet and how you like to use the Internet, you may like to use the Custom Level to define how IE is to respond to sites in each zone.

- **Active content** – Web designers may use small programs (applets), written in Java, Javascript or ActiveX to enhance their pages – though many are just decorative. The languages are designed to be secure – the programs should not be able to access your system – but hackers do find loopholes.

- **Privacy intrusions** – Every time you fill in a form online, run a search or make a choice, you send some information about yourself along with the intended data. Some sites may attempt to store and misuse this information.

- **Cookies** – A cookie is a short file, written by a site onto your hard disk. They are normally used to store your preferences at that site – so that when you revisit you don't have to set preferences again – or to log your visit. There are different sorts of cookies, some more intrusive than others. On the **Privacy** tab, you can set your limits for accepting cookies.

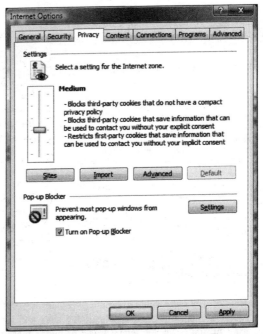

Figure 12.4 Using the Privacy tab to control cookies. The more you block, the safer you are, but some sites will not let you in if you block cookies. The Advanced options allow you to set up IE so that you can decide whether or not to accept cookies which would otherwise be blocked.

Content Advisor and safe surfing

If children can get online from your PC, you may want to enable the Content Advisor to set limits to the types of material that they can access through the Internet.

The Content Advisor allows you to restrict unsupervised access to those sites which have been rated by the Recreational Software Advisory Council for the Internet (RASCi). This rates sites on a scale of 1 to 5 for language, nudity, sex and violence. You set the limits of what may be accessed from your machine.

Many perfectly acceptable sites do not have a rating, simply because they not applied for one, but this is not a major problem. It just means that the kids will have to ask someone who knows the password to override the restrictions when they find somewhere good but unrated. And if you want to browse unrestricted, you can disable the advisor.

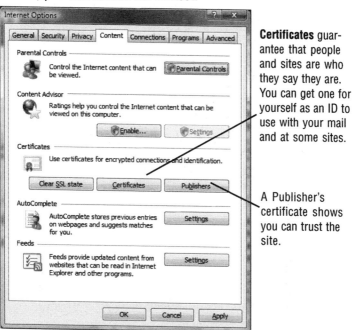

Certificates guarantee that people and sites are who they say they are. You can get one for yourself as an ID to use with your mail and at some sites.

A Publisher's certificate shows you can trust the site.

Figure 12.5 The Content tab. Turn on Content Advisor if you are going to let children have unsupervised access to the Internet. The Parental Controls button links to the standard Vista Parental Controls (page 138).

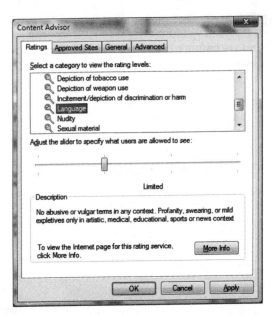

Figure 12.6 Defining what is acceptable. Note that these limits only apply to rated sites, and the majority of sites are unrated. On the General tab you can allow access to unrated sites, or supervised access to rated sites.

Safer surfing

If you are concerned about people reaching the murkier corners of the Internet, Content Advisor is only the first line of defence. For more about child safety, try these sites:

www.safekids.com.

www.child-internet-safety.com

www.childnet-int.org

Advanced

Most of the **Advanced** options should be left well alone until you really know what you are doing, but there are a couple that you might want to look at now.

In the **Accessibility** section, **Always expand ALT text for images** will make sure that there is enough space to display all the ALT text if **Show Pictures** has been turned off.

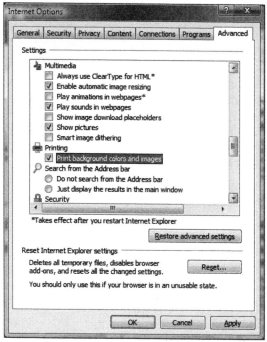

Figure 12.7 Most Advanced options should be left at their defaults – click Restore advanced settings if you think you may have messed them up!

At the bottom of the **Browsing** section, turn on **Use inline AutoComplete** if you want IE to try to finish URLs for you when you start typing them into the Address bar – this is a very handy facility.

In the **Multimedia** section, turn off the **Play** options for faster browsing.

12.5 Browsing the Web

Hyperlinks – addresses attached to text or images – provide an efficient means of following leads from page to page, but with so much information spread over so many pages on so many sites over the Web, the problem is where to start looking.

Your Internet Service Provider's home site will probably offer a directory with an organized set of links to selected sites, and

Internet Explorer is initially set up to head to MSN (MicroSoft Network). This has a good directory, so you may as well leave it as your start point until you have found a better place, then change to its address in the Internet Options dialog box (page 187).

A directory is good for starting research on general topics, but if you are looking for specific material, you are probably better off running a search, and with Internet Explorer you can run a search at any time, no matter where you are on the Web.

Running a search

1 In the Live Search box at the top right of the IE window, type a word or phrase to describe what you are looking for.

2 Press [Enter] or click 🔎.

3 When you get the results, click on a link to view the page.

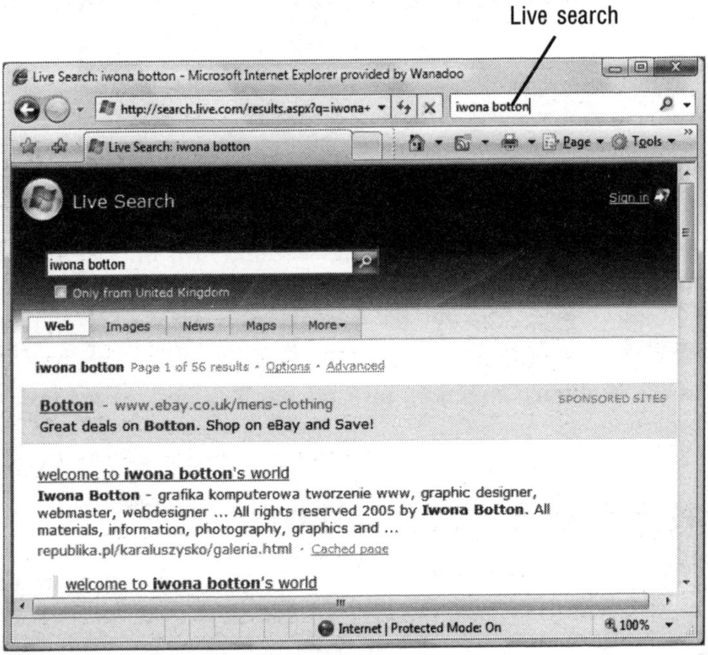

Live search

Figure 12.8 A search started in Internet Explorer is run at Live Search (though you can change to the search engine if you like). You are taken to the site for the results, and once there you can define your searches more closely, by selecting the types of results or by setting advanced options.

Other start points

There are many places that you can use as start points for your surfing. Some that are well worth a visit include:

◆ Yahoo!'s main site – the original and probably still the best of the directories, at

  http://www.yahoo.com

◆ Yahoo! UK & Ireland, at

  http://uk.yahoo.com

◆ Excite offers an excellent directory, search and more, at

  http://www.excite.co.uk

◆ The most comprehensive search engine is Google at

  http://www.google.com

But before you can get to these, you need to know about URLs. Read on!

Figure 12.9 There are local Yahoo!s in many countries, backed up by the central directory at www.yahoo.com. Yahoo! also offers web e-mail, news, weather, shopping and auctions, games, and more.

Uniform Resource Locators (URL)

With all the millions of web pages, files and other resources that can be reached over the Internet, a standardized way of identifying them is essential. URLs provide this. There are different styles of URL for each approach to the Internet, though they all follow much the same pattern:

type://hostcomputer/directory/filename

Web pages

Many of these are instantly recognizable from their *html* or *htm* endings, which shows that they are hypertext pages.

http://sunsite.unc.edu/boutell/faq/www-faq.html

This one is a list of frequently asked questions (*faq*) and their answers, about the World Wide Web (*www*), stored in the Sun archives in the University of North Carolina (*unc*).

The URL of the top page of a site may just consist of the site address, with an (optional) slash at the end. This is the opening page at Microsoft's site:

http://www.microsoft.com/

If you know the URL of a page, you can jump directly to it. Use **File → Open**, and type the URL into the panel, or type it into the **Address** toolbar.

The leading **http://** is not really necessary. The browser expects you to enter a World Wide Web URL. Thus:

http://uk.yahoo.com

can be entered as:

uk.yahoo.com

URLs must be typed exactly right or they will not work. They are not usually case-sensitive (though a few are) but do watch out for symbols. Where a URL is to the top page of a site, it may end in a slash (/). This can be omitted.

History

When you want to return to a page, the simplest way is through the Back button and the list that drops down from it. This only works with those visited very recently – the Back list is wiped at the end of a session, and can be corrupted by movements within sites, especially those with complex, interactive page layouts. The most reliable way to revisit pages is by opening the History list in the Favorites Center – use **Tools → Toolbars → History** to open it. The pages are grouped by day and then by site, making it easy to find the one you want.

Figure 12.10 Using the History list. Pages are grouped into their sites.

Favorites

The Favorites Center can also display the Favorites list. This comes with a few sets of ready-made links, but is really intended as a store of links to places that you like to revisit regularly.

◆ When you find a page that you will want again in future, open the **Favorites** menu and select **Add to Favorites** or open **Favorites** in the Favorites Center and click .

- Edit the name, if necessary – the page's title will be suggested.

- If you want to store the link in a folder, open the **Create in:** list and choose it – a new folder can be created, if needed.

- Click **Add**.

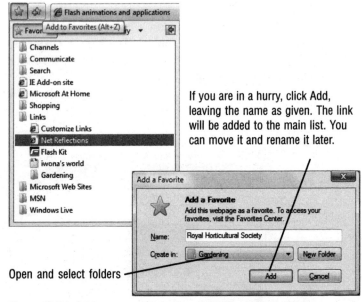

If you are in a hurry, click Add, leaving the name as given. The link will be added to the main list. You can move it and rename it later.

Open and select folders

Figure 12.11 Adding a page to the Favorites. If – more likely when – your Favorites folders get crowded and messy, use the menu command Favorites → Organize Favorites to open a display of the folders. You can then move, rename, delete and generally sort out your stored links.

12.6 Files from the Net

Shareware sites

The Internet is a great source of software – particularly for software that you can use on the Internet – but it's also a great source games, music, videos, pictures, text files and more.

If you are looking for shareware, try these excellent sites, both run by clnet – shareware.com (**http://www.shareware.com**) and download.com (**http://www.download.com**). Here you can search by keyword or program, or browse by category. When you find something that you want, clicking on the program's name will start the download – decide which folder to store it in, and sit back and wait. On a broadband connection, you should be able to download 2MB or more in a minute.

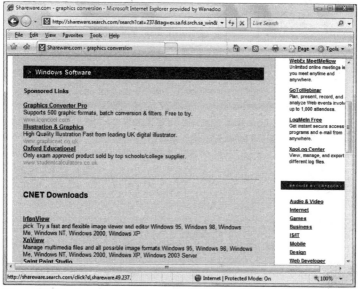

Figure 12.12 shareware.com – a great source of software. Some of it is free, the rest is shareware – try it for free, but pay to continue using it.

ZIPped files

Many of the files available online are compressed to save space. This reduces file sizes, and transfer times, by up to 90%. Zipped files can be opened in Windows Explorer.

Saving Web pages

You can revisit a page, offline, for as long as it is kept in the temporary files area, but if you want a permanent copy of a page you should save it.

* Wait until the page is fully loaded, then open the **File** menu and select **Save As** – you may need to change the filename to

something memorable. If you set the **Save as type** to *Web Page complete*, any images and the component files of framed pages are saved in a folder with the same name as the page.

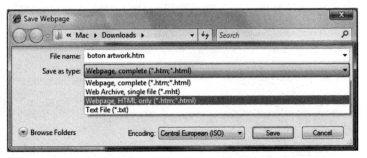

Figure 12.13 Saving a Web page. If you just want the text of a simple page (but with its formatting and layout), set the Save as type to 'Web Page, HTML only'.

♦ When you want to view the page again, use **File → Open**, then browse through your folders to locate it.

Saving text

The text of a Web page can be saved in two ways.

♦ If you want all of the text on the page, use **File → Save As**, and set the type to *Text File*.

♦ To save a chunk of the text, select it, use **Edit → Copy**, and paste it into a word-processor, then save it from there.

Saving images

If you don't want the whole page, but just an individual image from it, this can be saved separately.

♦ Point anywhere on the picture and wait for the image toolbar to appear, then click the **Save this image** button.

♦ If you really like the image and it is big enough to make a good background for your Desktop, right-click on it and select **Set as background** from the short menu.

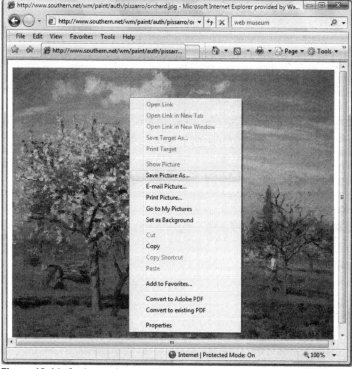

Figure 12.14 Saving an image off a Web page. This is from the Web Museum which has good quality images of many great paintings – you could download one and set it as the background to the Desktop. You can view the Musueum at many sites, including http://www.southern.net/wm

Windows Update

Windows Vista comes with an automatic update system. This will check the Microsoft website regularly, when you are online, to see if there are updates available that you should have. If there are, the system will download and install them for you. You don't need to do anything about this – it just happens!

• If you prefer to control when and how your Windows Vista software is updated, you can turn this facility off – open **Automatic Updates** in the Control Panel and switch to manual control.

If you choose to update manually, or want to see what optional updates are available, click on the **Windows Update** shortcut on the main **Start** menu. This is a highly automated page. It has routines that will check over your system to see if there are any files for which new replacements or 'patch' repairs are available. If there are any – or if you find any optional add-ons that you would like – they will be downloaded and installed for you.

If you have an Ultimate edition of Windows, you will also find extra goodies here from time to time. Keep visiting!

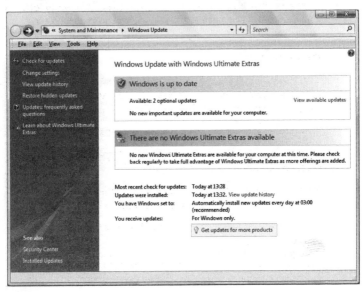

Figure 12.15 The Windows Update page.

Summary

* The Internet is the result of world-wide cooperation between computer networks in commercial, educational and other organizations.

* Getting online is simple with Windows Vista, especially with a braodband connection.

* Internet Explorer is an integral part of Windows Vista.

* Some of the Internet options should be set early on; others can be left until you have spent more time online.

* If children can get online from your PC, you should enable the Content Advisor.

* Directories help you find your way around; Yahoo! is the most comprehensive of these. Search engines can be used to track down pages containing keywords.

* You can search from the Live Search box in Explorer.

* The Web consists of pages linked together by URLs given as hyperlinks in the pages.

* Every site on the Internet has its own unique address. If you know the URL of a page, you can jump directly to it.

* The Favorites Center can be used to display the History or Favorites folders.

* Files can be downloaded from many places on the Net – shareware sites hold stores of free and cheap software.

* A Web page can be saved as a file. Text and pictures can also be saved separately.

* Use Windows Update to keep your system up to date.

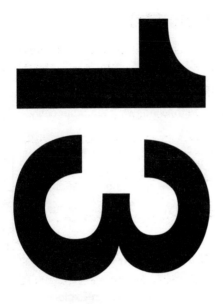

13 windows mail

In this chapter you will learn:

- about the Windows Mail screen
- how to read your mail
- how to create messages
- about the options
- how to use the Contacts lists

13.1 Starting Windows Mail

Windows Mail can be started from the Desktop icon or the **Start** menu, where it is fixed on the top left. The initial screen should have the Folder List to the left of the main pane, with the usual toolbar and menu bar above. There are alternative displays – reach them through the **View → Layout** command.

*   The **Folder List** shows the folders in which messages are stored, and is used for navigating between them.

*   The **Header Pane** lists the essential details of the messages in the selected folder.

*   The **Preview Pane** shows the message selected in the Header Pane.

*   The **Folder Bar** gives a pretty heading (it doesn't do anything).

*   The **View Bar** gives you a quick way to hide messages which have already been read.

The Folders

At first, there are only six mail folders. More can be created to provide organized storage for any mail messages and newsgroups that you join.

*   The **Inbox** holds mail sent to you. The messages remain here, after reading, until you move or delete them.

*   The **Outbox** provides temporary storage for messages, while they are waiting to be sent. If you have a dial-up line, and pay by the minute for access, it makes sense to compose your messages offline, and only go online to send them and collect incoming mail.

*   The **Sent** folder keeps a copy of outgoing messages, if you choose to keep copies (see page 210).

*   **Deleted Items** is where messages and articles are stored when they are first deleted. They are only removed completely when deleted from here.

*   Use **Drafts** as a temporary store for messages that you want to work on some more before sending.

Folder Bar   Header Pane   View Bar

          Folder List   Preview Pane

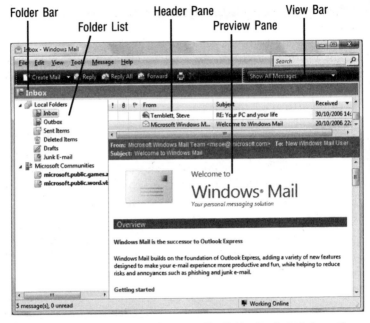

Figure 13.1 The Windows Mail screen. The Folder Bar is just decorative and you may find the View Bar useful. The View → Columns... option lets you select which items to display in the headers, but From, Subject and Received are generally enough to be able to find and sort messages.

- **Junk E-mail** is where Windows Mail puts those incoming messages which it thinks are junk. If you have a good ISP, and if you don't publish your e-mail address – tell it to your friends, but not to the world – then you shouldn't get too much junk.

13.2 Reading mail

Start by selecting the Inbox folder – if it is not already selected – to display its message headers. These show the name of the sender, the subject and when the message was received. They are normally in date order, but can be sorted by sender, subject or date, by clicking on the column name. If the message has not yet been read, its header will be in **bold**. When you select a header, the message is displayed in the preview pane (or in a separate window, if you have chosen this option).

When a message is displayed, these tools are available for dealing with it:

Reply – opens the New Message window, with the sender's name in the **To:** slot, ready to send back to them. This is neat as it means that you do not have to think about their e-mail address.

Reply to all – use this instead of Reply where a message has been mailed to a group of people, and you want your reply to reach the whole group! Your reply will then be mailed to all those who received a **To:** or **Cc:** copy (page 208) of the message.

Forward – copies the message into the New Message window, so that you can send it on to another person. This time you will have to supply the address, just as if you were sending a new message – see below.

Delete – moves the message to the Deleted folder. You can get Windows Mail to empty the Deleted folder for you on exit, or let them stay there, where they can be recovered if necessary – as with the Recycle Bin – until you delete them from there.

- You can also drag a message, at any time, from the header list to another folder for storage.

When people send you mail, it is stored in your mailbox at your Internet service provider.

If you have an always-on broadband connection, you can set up the options (page 209), so that Windows Mail checks the box and downloads new messages for you at set intervals.

If you have a dial-up connection, you can go online to pick up mail, and send messages in the Outbox, whenever it suits you.

Click **Send/Receive** to send and receive all your mail, or drop down its list (or open the **Tools** menu) if you only want to **Send** or to **Receive** at that time.

Send/Receive	
Send and Receive All	**Ctrl+M**
Receive All	
Send All	
pop.freeserve.com (Default)	

13.3 Sending mail

Windows Mail, like most modern mail software, can handle messages in HTML format (as used on Web pages), as well as plain text. This means that you can use different fonts, sizes and colours for your text, set bulleted or numbered lists and other layout options, and insert pictures. If you want colourful messages, without the bother of formatting them, there are a dozen Stationery styles. These give you decorative backgrounds and some also have matching text formats already set.

To write and send a message:

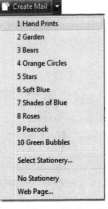

1 Click the **Create Mail** button, or use the command **Message ➜ New Message**.

Or

2 To use stationery, open the **Create Mail** drop-down list and pick a style.

   If you decide later that you don't like the style, use **Format ➜ Apply Stationery** in the New Message window to choose another style or revert to a plain background.

3 When the New Message window opens, type the recipient's e-mail address into the **To:** box, or click **To:** and select it from your Contacts list (see page 214 for more on this).

4 If more than one person is to get a copy, add addresses in the **To:** box (separated by semicolons or commas), or put them in the **Cc:** or **Bcc:** boxes.

   To: the main recipients – you would normally expect to get replies from these people.

   Cc: Carbon copies, sent mainly for information.

   Bcc: Blind carbon copies – their names will not appear in the lists of recipients that normally accompany each message. Used for circulating mail to large groups.

5 Type a **Subject** for the message, so that the recipients know what it is about when they see the header.

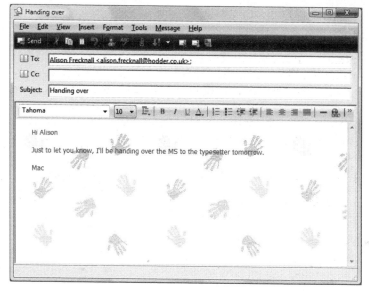

Figure 13.2 Composing a message using the Hand Prints stationery – apply formats as in normal word-processing.

6 Type and format your message. If you don't have the spell checker set to run automatically, you should read the message through to check for errors.

7 Click the **Send** button. If the spell checker is turned on, it will now run. After you have worked through any errors it finds, the message will be sent immediately, or stored in the Outbox to be sent later – it depends on the settings (see below).

Or

8 If you want to override your default send settings, open the **File** menu and select **Send Message** (i.e. now) or **Send Later**.

13.4 Windows Mail options

As with most software, the optional settings make more sense after you have been using it for a while, and the defaults are usually a safe bet to start with. However, there are a few that are worth checking and setting early on. Use **Tools ➞ Options...** to open the **Options** panel.

The **General** tab deals with the interaction between Windows Mail and your system.

- Turn on *Check for new messages every ?? minutes*, and set the interval, if you are always online.

- Turn off *Notify me if there are any new newsgroups* if you don't bother with the news.

- All the other options are probably best turned on at this stage.

The **Read** tab is mainly concerned with news articles.

- Some groups have hundreds of articles every day. You can set how many headers to download at a time.

- Where a set of articles has the same Subject (follow-ons start with 'Re:') they are grouped. If *Automatically expand grouped messages* is off, only the first is shown until you click ⊞.

The **Receipts** tab set how to deal with receipts. You can request them when sending messages, and people may ask you for them.

The **Send** tab is mainly about message formats (see Figure 13.3).

- Turn on *Save copy of sent messages* only if you normally need to keep a copy for later reference.

- Turn on *Send messages immediately* if you normally deal with your mail online.

- Turning on *Automatically put people I reply to in my Contacts list* is a good idea. It ensures that their address is correct – as it has been copied from their mail. If this includes some people you do not want, they can easily be removed.

- The *Include message in reply* option can be useful, especially if most of your e-mail is work-related. When replying, you can edit out any unwanted bits of the original message.

- Set your **Mail Sending Format** to *HTML* if most of your recipients are able to read HTML formatted messages, but select *Plain Text* for News.

The **Compose** tab lets you define your message format, setting the default fonts and stationery.

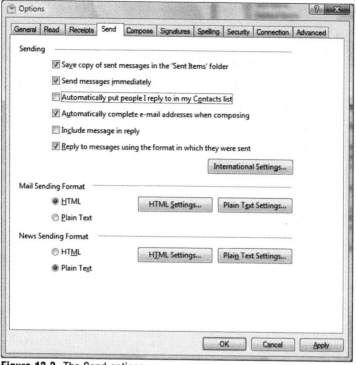

Figure 13.3 The Send options.

Signatures are short files that can be attached to the end of every message. Poeple use them to add their other contact details, or – in companies – to carry disclaimers that the views expressed are those of the sender, not the firm. They are entirely optional.

The **Spelling** tab controls the way that the spell checker works. The main option is *Always check spelling before sending* – turn this on or off. Other options let you select the dictionary and define the kind of words that the spell checker should ignore.

The **Security** tab should be left alone for the time being – and can be ignored if you are not worried about the security of your mail.

The **Connection** tab controls when and how you go online and off again. If things are working nicely, leave this alone.

The **Advanced** tab options can be left at their defaults, but click the **Maintenance** button and set how to clean up messages.

- Turn on *Empty messages from the Deleted Items folder on exit* unless you tend to delete items in error. If this is off, you will have to delete the messages again to remove them.

- Compacting the database does not delete messages, but stores them more efficiently.

- The remaining options refer to newsgroup messages. How long – if at all – do you want to keep old articles? Remember that they can be copied to other folders for storage.

- The **Troubleshooting** options can be turned on if you have problems with your mail or news. The log files could provide useful information for whoever tries to solve the problems.

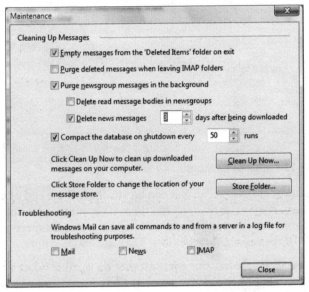

Figure 13.4 Cleaning up messages doesn't just save space – not a problem with big hard disks – it makes it easier to find the stuff you want.

13.5 Windows Contacts

You must get e-mail addresses exactly right, or the post won't get through. Unfortunately, addresses are not always user-friendly and are rarely easy to remember. The Contacts is the solution – once you have a correct e-mail address in here you need never worry about it again. When you want to write to someone, you can select the name from the book and start to compose from there, or start the message and then select the names at the **To:** and **Cc:** boxes.

Windows Contacts is a separate program, though designed to work closely with Windows Mail. You can open Contacts from Mail, and start from Contacts and send a message through Mail.

Figure 13.5 My Contacts list – you can store phone numbers and 'snail mail' address details here as well.

Adding to the Contacts

If you turn on the option to put people you reply to in your Contacts list (page 210), then you will rarely need to add them by hand – but it is as well to know how.

1 Open **Windows Contacts** from the **Tools** menu.

2 Click the **New Contact** button. There are tabs for lots of information, but only the **Name** tab is essential.

3 The First, Middle and Last names should be entered separately if you want to be able to sort the list by First and Last names. (**View → Sort By** has a number of alternative sort orders – very useful when you have lots of entries.)

4 A **Nickname** can be entered, if wanted, and either this or the full name can be set as the **Display** value.

5 Type the address *carefully* into the **E-mail address:** box, and click **Add**. If the person has more than one e-mail address, add the others then select one as the default.

6 Switch to the other tabs to enter more details if required, then click **OK**.

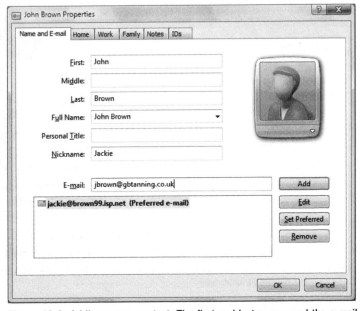

Figure 13.6 Adding a new contact. The first and last names and the e-mail address are the only essentials, and are quickly added.

Using the Contacts list

If the Contacts list is open already, you can start a new message to someone by selecting their name and clicking on their address. The **New Message** window will open, with the name in the **To:** box.

If you start from the New Message button, click the ▣ To: icon to open the **Select Recipients** panel. This lists the names in your Address Book. Pick the recipients one at a time, clicking ⎡To: ->⎤ .

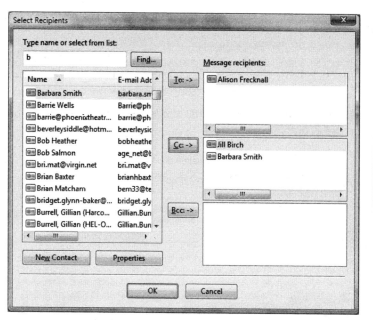

Figure 13.7 Using the Select Recipients panel to get addresses from your Contacts list. If you add a name by mistake, select it and press [Delete].

Cc -> or Bcc -> to copy them to the appropriate categories. Click OK when you've done. The recipients will appear as names, rather than e-mail addresses – don't worry. They will be translated into addresses before sending.

13.6 Files by mail

Files of any type – graphics, word-processor and spreadsheet documents, audio and video clips – and URL links, can be attached to messages and sent by e-mail. Compared to sending files printed or on disk in the post, e-mail is almost always quicker, often more reliable and cheaper.

- If you use the Rich Text (HTML) format, rather than plain text, you can also insert pictures directly into a message.

1 Compose the message.

- To attach a file

2 From the **Insert** menu select **File Attachment**...

3 Browse for the file and click **Open**.

- To insert a picture

4 Open the **Format** menu and select **Rich Text**.

5 From the **Insert** menu select **Picture**...

6 Browse for the picture source and click **Open**.

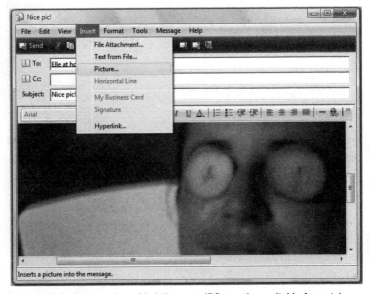

Figure 13.8 Pictures (provided they are JPG or other suitable formats) can be displayed in messages. Any kinds of files can be attached.

Detaching files

Detaching files from messages used to be hard work – they had to be cut out from the text of the message and processed through special decoding software. With Windows Mail, it's a piece of cake. If the preview pane header bar is present, an attached file is shown by a paperclip icon. If it is not, you must open the message in its own window – the file will be listed in the Attach: line.

1 Click on the icon to open the menu.

2 Click on the name and the file will be opened in its linked application.

3 The system may check that you want to open the file – click **Open** if you are sure that it is safe.

Or

4 Select **Save Attachments** and save the file to disk.

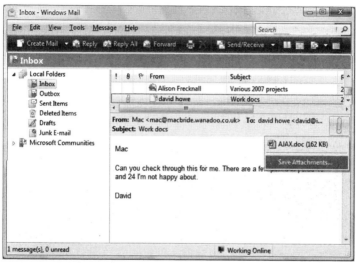

Figure 13.9 Attached files can be opened from within the message or saved to disk.

Newsgroups and communities

What Windows Mail refers to as communities used to be called newsgroups, and they were once the main way in which people came together online to share interests and enthusiasms. Newsgroups were where you could ask for and give help, debate and announce new discoveries and ideas. At the peak there were over 50,000 each devoted to a different topic, from the seriously academic to the totally trivial. Newsgroups still exist, and some have large and active memberships, but their role has largely been replaced by blogs and chat rooms. Dip into the communities sometime, to see if there is anything there for you.

Summary

* Windows Mail handles mail through a set of folders. The key ones are the Inbox, where incoming mail is stored, and the Outbox, where messages collect ready for sending.

* The subjects in the header lines should give you an idea of the nature of a message. You can easily reply to, or forward on, incoming mail.

* When composing a new message, you can use Stationery and apply formats to the text.

* Messages can be sent immediately, or stored and sent later when you go online.

* The Options control your interaction with the system, and how and when messages are sent and read.

* Use the Contacts list to store the e-mail addresses of your contacts, and you will only have to type an address once!

* Files can be attached to messages and sent by e-mail. Files attached to incoming messages can be opened or saved.

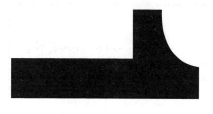

accessories

In this chapter you will learn:

- how Windows Vista works
- about what's on the screen
- how to respond to and control Vista
- some essential terminology

14.1 WordPad

Don't underrate WordPad just because it's free. It has all the facilities that you would have found in the top-flight software a few years ago, and compares well with today's commercial packages. It's fine for writing letters, essays, reports, source code for computer programs and anything else where you want to be able to edit text efficiently, format it with different fonts, styles and colours, and perhaps incorporate graphics or other files.

* When entering text, just keep typing when you reach the edge of the page – the text will be wrapped round to the next line. Only press the **Enter** key at the end of a paragraph.

Standard toolbar – with the main filing and editing tools

Formatting toolbar   Ruler

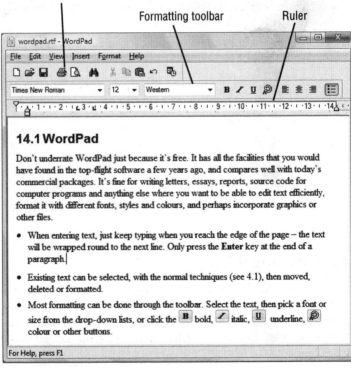

Figure 14.1 WordPad, being used to create the text for these pages! Notice that images can be embedded in the text. They can also be inserted as free-standing images.

- Existing text can be selected, with the normal techniques (see section 4.1), then moved, deleted or formatted.

- Most formatting can be done through the toolbar. Select the text, then pick a font or size from the drop-down lists, or click the **B** bold, *I* italic, <u>U</u> underline, colour or other buttons.

- The ☰ left, ☰ centre and ☰ right alignment buttons determine how the text lines up with the edges of the paper.

- The ☷ bullets button indents text from the left, with a blob at the start of each paragraph.

- Alignment and bullet formats apply to whole paragraphs. You do not need to select the whole paragraph – if the cursor is within it, or part of its text is selected, the paragraph will be formatted.

Indents and tabs

These are best set from the ruler. Select the text where new indents or tabs are required then drag the icons to set the indent; click to set a tab point.

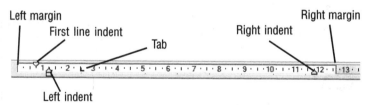

Left margin   Right margin
   First line indent   Right indent
                 Tab
Left indent

Full font formatting

Though you can set almost all font options from the toolbar buttons, you get better control through the **Font** panel – open it with **Format → Font**. Here you can set all aspects of the selected text, and preview the effects of your choices. Watch the **Sample** text as you change the settings.

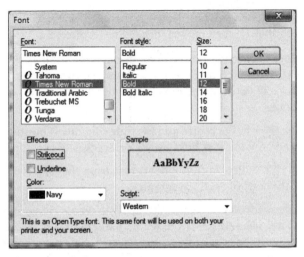

Figure 14.2 The Font dialog box. You'll find similar panels in all applications that use fonts. Click OK when you like the look of the Sample.

Page Setup

The **Page Setup** panel, opened from the **File** menu option, controls the basic size and layout of the page – for all pages in the document.

- The **Paper Size** and **Source** settings rarely need changing – if you've set your printer properties correctly. If you are printing on card or special paper, change the **Source** to *Manual*, if the option is available.

- In the **Orientation** area, *Portrait* is the normal way up; use *Landscape* if you want to print with the paper sideways.

- The **Margins** set the overall limits to the printable area. You can use the indents to reduce the width of text within the margins, but you cannot extend out beyond them.

- Click the **Printer** button to reach its **Properties** panel to change any settings at that level – you might, for example, want to switch to a lower resolution for printing a draft copy, or a higher resolution for the final output. (At low resolution, the printer will work faster and use less ink or toner.)

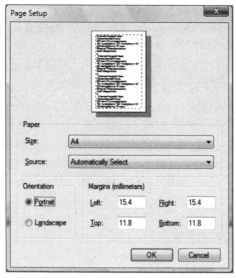

Figure 14.3 The Page Setup panel in WordPad. Measurements here are in millimetres, but can be changed on the View → Options panel.

Graphics and other objects

Pictures, graphs, spreadsheets, audio and video clips – in fact just about any object that can be produced by any Windows application – can be incorporated into a WordPad document.

1 From the **Insert** menu select **Object...**

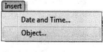

2 If the object does not exist, pick **Create New**, select the **Object Type** and click **OK**. The appropriate application will open. When you have

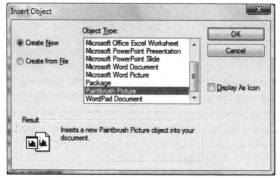

created the object, save it if you want to keep a separate copy for future use, then select the **Exit & Return to Document** option from the **File** menu.

3 If you want to use an existing object, select **Create from File**, and browse through your folders to locate it.

4 Back in WordPad, you can move or resize the object. Select it – it will be outlined with handles at the corners and edges.

Point to a handle to get the double-headed arrow then drag in or out as required. The position of the object across the page can be set by using the alignment buttons.

Figure 14.4 Adjusting the size of an image in WordPad. An inserted object can be edited by double-clicking on it – this opens the source application. Use Exit & Return when you have finished editing.

You can't do fancy layouts with WordPad. An image can sit by itself, separate from the text above and below, or can be embedded in a single line. That's it.

Print Preview

Like almost all applications, WordPad has a Print Preview facility. Working on screen, it can be difficult to tell how a document will look on paper – you may not be able to see the full width of the page and you certainly won't be able to see the full height. Use the Preview to get a better idea of the printed output, before you commit it to paper. Are your images or headings large enough to make the impact that you want? Do you get awkward breaks in the text at the ends of pages? If you are happy with the look of your document, you can print from here by clicking the **Print** button, otherwise, click **Close** to return to WordPad for further tweaking.

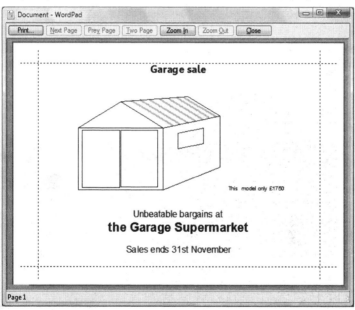

Figure 14.5 Using the Print Preview facility to check the overall layout of a page. You can print from here, or close to return to editing.

Saving and opening files

In WordPad as in all applications you should save early and save often! Don't wait until you have finished writing that eight-page report before you save it. Applications can crash, hardware can fail, plugs get knocked out and we all make mistakes! The first save may take a few moments, but later saves are done at the click of a button.

To save a file for the first time:

1 Open the **File** menu and select **Save As...**

2 If the folder shown at the top is not the one you want to use, click **Browse Folders** to open the full dialog box.

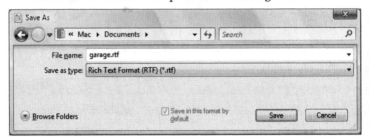

3 Navigate through the Folder list and Contents Pane to select the folder.

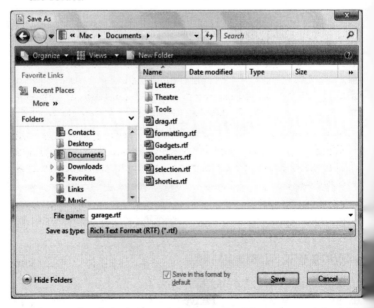

4 Change the default 'Document' in the filename to something that will remind you what it is about.

5 RTF is the standard WordPad format – it can be read by many applications. If you want to save in a different format, pick one from the **Save as type** drop-down list.

6 Click **Save**.

♦ To resave the current document after you have done more work on it, click 🔳 – that's it!

When you close the document or exit from WordPad, if you have not saved the document in its final state, you will be prompted to do so.

Next time that you want to work on the document, open it from the **File** menu. Either:

♦ Select **Open** and then browse for the file – the dialog box is used in the same way as the Save As dialog box.

♦ If it is one of the files that you have used most recently, it will be listed at the bottom of the **File** menu. Just select it from here.

14.2 Character Map

You will find **Character Map** on the **System Tools** menu – don't ask me why! It's a useful tool and one that I like to have close to hand. It allows you to see the characters available in any font, and to copy individual characters from there into a document.

1 Pick a font from the drop-down list – Symbol, Webdings and Wingdings are the main fonts for decorative characters, and you will find foreign letters and mathematical symbols in most other fonts.

2 Click on the character for an enlargement – if you hold down the left mouse button and move across the characters, enlargements will appear as you go.

3 To copy characters into a document, click **Select** – the current one will be added to the **Characters to copy** display – then click **Copy** when you have all you want. Return to your document and use **Edit → Paste** – the character(s) will be copied in, formatted to the chosen font.

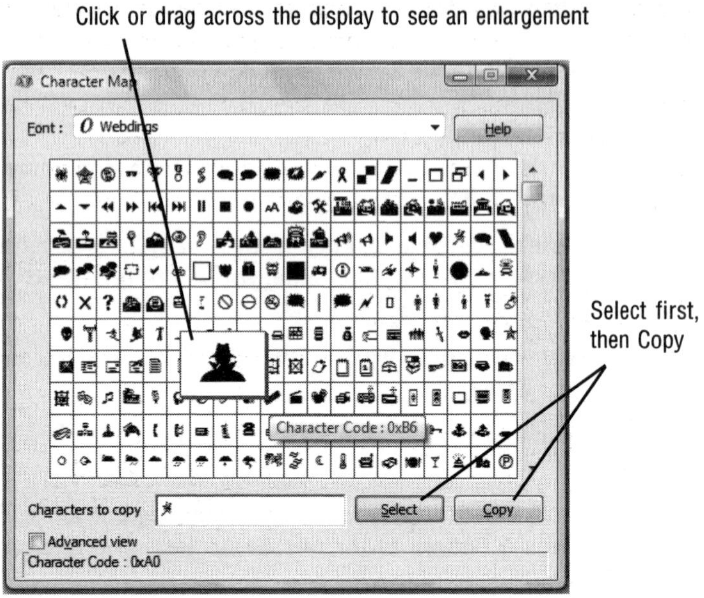

Click or drag across the display to see an enlargement

Select first, then Copy

Character Code : 0xB6

Characters to copy 　

Select 　 Copy

Advanced view

Character Code : 0xA0

Figure 14.6 Character Map.

If you also find that Character Map is a useful tool to have at hand, open the Start menu and drag it from the System Tools folder into the main program list, or create a shortcut to it on your Desktop.

14.3 Paint

Graphics software falls into two broad groups. The first type works with objects – lines, circles, text boxes, etc. – that remain separate, and can be moved, deleted, recoloured and otherwise changed at any point. Word's Drawing facility works this way.

In the second type, which includes Paint, the image is produced by applying colour to a background – with each new line overwriting anything that may be beneath. Using these is very like real painting. You may be able to wipe out a mistake while the paint is still wet, but as soon as it has dried it is fixed on the canvas. (Paint allows you to undo the last move.) I use Pain regularly – it's ideal for trimming and tidying screenshots for books, though I don't expect many of you will want it for this purpose. Though it can be used to produce intricate images, these can be created more successfully on a computer art package, with a full set of shading, shaping and manipulating tools. Paint is probably best used to draw simple diagrams, or as a children's toy, or to get an idea of how this type of graphics software works.

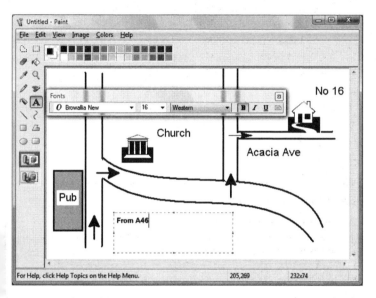

Figure 14.7 Using Paint to create a diagram. The **Text toolbar** gives you the full range of fonts and the main style effects.

The Toolbox

There is a simple but adequate set of tools. A little experimentation will show how they all work.

Most of them have options that can be set in the area below the toolbar.

◆ When you select an area (or paste an image from file or from the Clipboard) the background can be transparent or opaque.

◆ You can set the size of the Eraser, Brush, Airbrush, Line and Curve. N.B. the Line thickness applies to the closed shapes.

Free-Form select			Select rectangle
Eraser			Fill with colour
Pick Colour			Magnifier
Pencil			Brush
Airbrush			Text
Line			Curve
Closed shapes {	Rectangle		Polygon
	Oval		Rounded rectangle
Transparent background			
Opaque background			Option area

+ The Magnifier is 4× by default, but can be 2×, 6× or 8×.

+ The Pencil is only ever 1 pixel wide.

+ Closed shapes can be outline or fill only, or both.

The Curve is probably the trickiest of the tools to use. The line can have one or two curves to it.

1 Draw a line between the points where the curve will start and end.

2 Drag to create the first curve – exaggerate the curve as it will normally be reduced at the next stage.

3 If the line is to have a second curve, drag it out now – as long as the mouse button is down, the line will flex to follow the cursor.

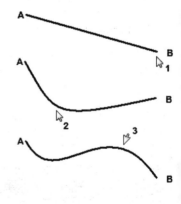

4 For a simple curve, just click at the end of the line.

Undo it!

If you go wrong any time – and you will with the Curve – use **Edit → Undo**. This removes the effect of the last action.

Working with selected areas

The rectangular and free-form selectors can be used to select an area of the screen. Once selected, an area can be:

+ Deleted – use this for removing mistakes and excess bits.

+ Copied – handy for creating repeating patterns.

+ Saved as a file – use **Edit → Copy To...** and give a filename.

+ Dragged elsewhere on screen.

+ Flipped (mirrored) horizontally or vertically, or rotated in 90° increments – use **Image → Flip/Rotate** for these effects.

+ Stretched – to enlarge, shrink or distort, or skewed, either horizontally or vertically – use **Image → Stretch/Skew**.

Colours

The colour palette is used in almost the same way in all Windows programs. You can select a colour from the basic set – use the left button for the foreground colour and the right button for the background – or you can mix your own colours.

Double-click on a colour in the **Color Box** or use **Colors → Edit Colors** to open the **Edit Colors** panel. Initially only the **Basic**

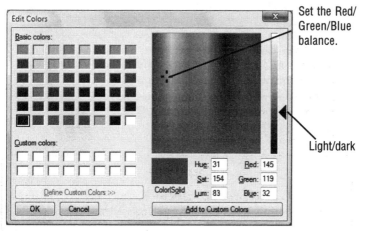

Set the Red/ Green/Blue balance.

Light/dark

Figure 14.8 Editing colours in Paint.

colors will be visible. Click **Define Custom Colors** to open the full panel.

To define a new colour, drag the cross-hair cursor in the main square to set the Red/Green/Blue balance and move the arrow up or down the right-hand scale to set the light/dark level. Colours can also be set by typing in values, but note that you are mixing light, not paint. Red and green make yellow; red, green and blue make grey/white; the more you use, the lighter the colour.

When you have the colour you want, click **Add to Custom Colors**. The new colour will replace the one currently selected in the Color Box on the main screen.

Filing

Saving and opening files is the same here as in WordPad. You can also use **Edit ➔ Copy To...** to save part of an image and **Edit ➔ Paste From...** to open a file so that you can combine its image with the existing picture. The image will come in as a selected area, which can be positioned wherever required. Set the background to transparent to merge the two images, or to opaque for the new file to overlay the old image.

Screenshots

If you press the [Print Screen] key, the whole screen display will be copied into the Clipboard. If you press [Alt] + [Print Screen] then only the active window will be copied. The image can then be pasted into Paint, or any other graphics program, and saved from there. That's how most of the screenshots were produced for this book.

14.4 The Snipping Tool

Here is an alternative to Print Screen and Paint. Snip allows you to capture images – the whole screen, a window, any rectangular section, or an irregular shape defined by hand. You can then add highlights or drawn lines on the captured image before saving it or sending off by e-mail. The ability to capture a defined area, and to add highlights, could be useful at times.

To capture a screenshot:

1 In the **Start** menu, open the **Accessories** folder and select **Snipping Tool**.

2 Click the arrow beside **New** and select the **Snip** mode from the drop-down list. Then ...

3 With a **Rectangular** or **Free-form Snip**, use the mouse to define the area to be captured.

4 With a **Window Snip**, click on the window to be captured.

5 With a **Full-screen Snip** the screen is snipped immediately.

6 In the Snipping Tool window, use the **Highlighter**, **Pen** or **Eraser** as required to identify or edit points of interest.

7 Click the tools or use **File ➜ Save As**, to store the image, or **File ➜ Send To**, to pass it to someone else.

8 Click the **New** tool or use **File ➜ New** to capture another.

Snip Options

If you are going to use Snip regularly, check the Options and make sure that it is working the way that suits you best.

Copy
Colour choice

Save As   Pen   Highlighter
New   Send To   Eraser

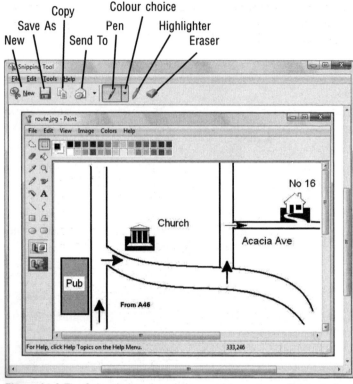

Figure 14.9 The Snip window, here being used to capture a Paint window.

14.5 Calculator

Pack away that pocket calculator. You don't need it on your desk now that you have one on your Desktop!

The Calculator can work in two modes – Standard or Scientific – use the View menu options to switch between them.

In either mode, use this as if it was a hand-held calculator. Enter the numbers, arithmetic operators and functions by clicking on the screen keys, or from your keyboard. (You can still use the keyboard when in the Scientific mode as there are keyboard shortcuts for the extra buttons – look in the Help file for the list of 'keyboard equivalents of calculator buttons'.)

It has the same limitations as a pocket calculator – you can only store one value in memory at a time (**MS** to store it, **M+** to add to the value in memory, **MR** to recall it and **MC** to clear it); and you cannot print your results (though you can copy the result into another document). If you want more than this, use a spreadsheet!

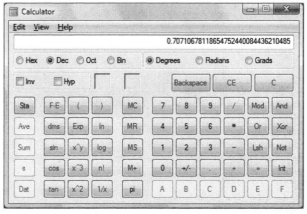

Figure 14.10 The Calculator in Scientific mode. In either mode, it works to 32-digit accuracy – is that close enough for you?

14.6 Photo Gallery

The Photo Gallery is the default viewer for photos and similar image files. And it is not just a viewer – you can also edit the image and add tags or change its star rating.

It has two modes:

* It can show the contents of a folder in almost exactly the same way as Windows Explorer. The main difference is that tags are also used to allocate images to folders.

* It can be used to view and edit a single image. The editing tools are limited, but may be enough to tweak photos before printing. You can adjust the exposure, colour balance and 'red eye', or crop out a section.

Fix = go to editing mode   Info = display file information

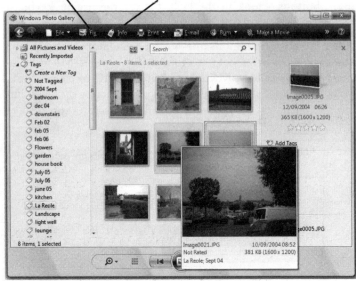

Figure 14.11 The Photo Gallery when exploring a folder ...

Revert to folder view

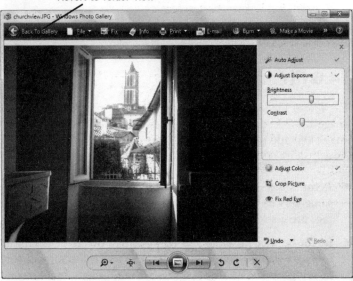

Figure 14.12 ... when working on one image – try Auto Adjust before fiddling with the adjustments yourself. It's good.

To start Photo Gallery:

1 Click on its entry in the Start menu, then select the folder.

Or

2 Open the folder in Explorer, then select any image, click the **Preview** button and select **Photo Gallery**.

14.7 Media Player

Media Player is a multi-purpose audio/video player. It can handle sound files in MIDI and in the native Windows format, WAVE – as well as audio CDs – or video in the standard Video for Windows (AVI), Media Audio/Video (WMA and ASF) or the many ActiveMovie formats.

If you simply want some music while you work, Media Player can play a CD for you.

◆ Put the CD into the drive and wait for a moment for Media Player to start up and to read in the track information. The CD will play the tracks in their playlist sequence – initially this will be the standard order.

Rip and Burn

But Media Player is more than just a player – it can also rip (copy music from a CD or video from a DVD) and burn (copy files onto a CD or DVD). At the simplest you could rip an entire CD onto your hard drive, then burn the tracks in their original order onto a blank CD, then wipe the files from your hard drive. But you aren't restricted to disk-to-disk copying. In between ripping tracks and burning them, you can edit the information, store the files on your hard drive and organize them how you like.

Respect copyright

As long as you have paid for an audio or video file, or if its authors have waived copyright, then you can make copies for your own use – but not for sale or rental or any other form of earning money.

Shuffle   Repeat   Play controls   Volume

Figure 14.13 Media Player ripping tracks from a CD.

To rip a CD:

1 Place the CD in the drive. Windows Media Player should start to play it automatically.

2 Clear the checkboxes for any tracks you do not want to rip.

3 Click the **Rip** button and set the format and bit rate.

4 Windows Media Audio is the default format. You also have:

Media Audio Pro is designed for use on mobile phones;

Media Audio variable bit rate produces smaller files but takes longer to rip;

Media Audio Lossless gives best quality sound, but at the cost of larger files;

MP3 and WAV formats are available if wanted.

5 Set the bit rate, as required – increasing the rate improves the sound quality and produces larger files.

6 Start the rip and wait. It'll take a while.

To edit the album information:

1 Click the Library button and select the album.

2 If Media Player cannot read the album and track information from the CD, you will have to supply them yourself. Click into an '**Unknown...**' box and type in the data.

Figure 14.14 Editing tracks – a necessity with older CDs. Newer ones and digital downloads carry their own album and track information.

To burn a CD:

1 Click the **Burn** button. A Burn List will appear at the bottom right of the window.

2 Drag tracks from the Library into the Burn List.

3 To change the order of tracks in the list, drag them up or down as required.

4 When you have all the tracks in place, click **Start Burn**.

Windows Media Center is a more sophisticated alternative to the Media Player. As well as playing CDs and DVDs, this can also play recorded TV, if the necessary video decoders and cards are present in the PC.

Figure 14.15 Adding tracks to the list before burning a CD.

Summary

* WordPad has enough formatting and layout facilities to cope with many word-processing jobs.

* Character Map will let you see characters in any font. You can copy them here and paste them into documents.

* Paint is a simple graphics program that can be used for creating diagrams, fun pictures and for editing and saving screenshots.

* The Snipping Tool is designed for capturing whole or partial screenshots.

* Calculator will do the job of a simple or a scientific pocket calculator.

* Use the Photo Gallery to view and edit your digital photographs.

* Media Player can play audio CDs, and audio and video files in most formats, and can rip and burn CDs.

index